# The Crisis
# in
# Christian
# Music

Printed in the United States of America

ISBN 1-57558-062-4

# The Crisis
# in
# Christian
# Music

Jack Wheaton

# Table of Contents

# Introduction

Bring no more vain oblations; incense is an abomination unto
me; the new moons and sabbaths, the calling of assemblies,
I cannot away with; it is iniquity, even the solemn meeting.
—Isaiah 1:13

Recently I accompanied Dr. Noah Hutchings, director of South-
west Radio Church and a leading Christian author, teacher,
and lecturer on an exciting trip to Israel and Jordan. We had
many interesting conversations, but one of the most interesting and continuous was our discussion of what can only be
called a "crisis" in Christian music.

Many Chrisitans, not only most of those over thirty, but
many sensitive young believers have either left a church,
stopped going to church, or are arriving at church late because
of the introduction of contemporary Christian music into the
worship service. The standard complaints are that a) the music is too loud, b) the music is repetitious, c) the instrumentation is more reflective of a rock band than a church ensemble,
d) the musicians are dressed like they are going trick-or-treat-
ing on Halloween rather than dressing up for church, and e)
the lyrics of the songs trivialize the basic standards of our faith
and create a false sense of familiarity with Jesus Christ and

the Holy Spirit.

In addition, many are concerned about the sudden jettisoning of almost two thousand years of spiritually tried-and-true hymns, choruses, anthems, and praise songs for something so worldly, so trivial, and so vain. On the other hand, many are claiming that the introduction of this style of worldly music into the church worship service is the only way to attract young people to attend church.

My professional training and background in music, history, and the Bible has led me to make a serious study of this problem and what can be done about it. I do not believe that the problem is unsolvable.

There are many spiritually and musically worthy contemporary praise songs that have been written in the past fifty years. We certainly do not wish to throw them out of the church. Still, this problem must be addressed and no longer avoided. It is seriously dividing the body of Christ, something our adversary, the Devil is delighted to see happening.

In this book we will examine the problem, the hidden power of music, and what can be done to correct the situation. Please encourage others in your church or music group to pick up a copy and begin applying these objective principles to solving the crisis in contemporary Christian music today.

> For God hath not given us the spirit of fear; but of power, and of love, and of a sound mind.
>
> —2 Timothy 1:7

# The Problem

A wonderful and horrible thing is committed in the land;
The prophets prophesy falsely, and the priests bear rule by
their means; and my people love to have it so: and what will
ye do in the end thereof?
                                                    —Jeremiah 5:30,31


Today there is a crisis in Christian music. Secular, pagan, and
even occult musical styles have crept into the church, all
dressed up with new Christian lyrics. Old, traditional hymns,
tried and true, have been thrown on the scrap heap of church
history.

Naively, pastors, music directors, and younger members
of congregations have often unknowingly embraced musical
styles that can have spiritually negative affects on their listeners. Music is so powerful it can easily overpower the higher
reasoning portions of the brain and bring about uncontrollable physiological, psychological, and spiritual changes that are
often in direct conflict with biblical teachings.

Christians used to concentrate on taking tried and true
spiritual formats, including sanctified music, into the world.
Today we invite the world system to enter, and sometimes
dominate, the church through its music.

It's not that most older and even many younger but spiritually sensitive parishoners resent the casual dress or the instrumentation found in the contemporary praise bands, which is often a direct copy of a rock band. It goes much deeper than that. There are definite physiological, psychological, and spiritual dangers tied up with the volume, the constant repetition, and the rhythms often used in contemporary Christian music.

In my ten-year study writing *All That Jazz: A History of Afro-American Music,* I discovered that music played a principle role in most of the pagan religions of Africa, many of which survived the crossing from Africa to the New World and remain alive today through occult religions in Cuba, Brazil, and other parts of Latin America. The purpose of certain rhythms and the constant repetition of phrases was to (a) call forth "spirits" (demonic forces), (b) put the congregation into a state of music-induced hypnosis, and (c) activate certain changes within the body that were beyond conscious control.

Today, I find that many of these same occultic musical styles have crept not only into American pop music, but are now standard practices in many of the contemporary Christian musical styles.

Is all contemporary Christian music bad? No! There have been many wonderful, inspirational, and devotional praise songs written within the last fifty years. We must not throw out the baby with the bath water, so to speak, when judging the affects of contemporary Christian music.

Fortunately, there are rather objective standards that can be applied when trying to decide what contemporary Christian music is fit for leading worship in a church, and which is not. These standards will be presented later in this book and can be used as an objective guideline for discerning and choosing the right music for the right occasion within the church.

I have tried to avoid a self-righteous approach in helping

to understand and solve the problems raised in this study. I have also tried to avoid making it a battle between the younger and the older members of our congregations. What I endeavored to do is warn the church that certain musical styles, performance practices, and rhythms — when introduced into worship services today — can have serious negative affects on the congregation and further divide the Body of Christ.

May God, our Lord Jesus Christ, and the Holy Spirit, always be our guide when choosing music for worship services. May we also be aware that our adversary, Satan, has found another way to slither in and compromise worship and the sanctity of the sanctuary through pagan musical styles.

> Take it back three or four thousand years — take it back to that cat who found a bone and beat the bone on the rock and started to yell at the full moon, and then you might have the original song — and that's rock 'n roll.
>
> —Keith Richards, guitarist for the Rolling Stones,
> from his autobiography *Keith*

# How Did it Get This Way?

Behold, this was the iniquity of thy sister Sodom, pride, fulness of bread, and abundance of idleness was in her and in her daughters, neither did she strengthen the hand of the poor and needy. And they were haughty, and committed abomination before me: therefore I took them away as I saw good.

—Ezekiel 16:49–50

### Introduction

Recently my wife and I visited a new local church. The pastor was teaching and preaching the Word of God in a timely and appropriate manner. His teaching was expositional, taking the congregation book-by-book through the Bible and explaining what difficult passages really meant and how to apply that teaching to our everyday life. Too many "modern" pastors today have drifted away from the Word of God, preferring instead to give "have a nice day" sermons with little or no scriptural references or interpretation of the deeper meanings found in the Word of God.

### Rock Format

We enjoyed the sermon, but the music, the worship service that precedes the message, was a disaster! Most of it was too loud, poorly played, and poorly sung. They sang contemporary Christian choruses (some of which I refer to as "bumpersticker" songs) that usually have inane lyrics which are repeated over and over. The accompanying ensemble was a typical rock ensemble: drums, electric bass, two guitars, and synthesizer. The "choir" was composed of four singers — two male, two female — all singing in unison, and often badly out of tune.

Even when a traditional hymn was sung, it was accompanied with a raucous rock beat, more suitable for a teenage dance, but certainly not appropriate for a worship service. To compound matters, the music was poorly prepared: unrehearsed, out-of-tune (in spots), and led enthusiastically by a music leader who (sadly) could not "sing" (by normal standards), but who obviously believed that he could. He certainly was enthusiastic about the public display of his vocal limitations.

The music worship part of the service seemed more like an amateur rock band contest at a junior high school than any attempt to lead the congregation in serious, holy worship of the one true God and His Son, Jesus Christ. How sad, but how accommodating were the parishioners!

## Worship?

As I looked around the room, those present who were over thirty-five years of age were grimacing, clapping hands halfheartedly, and mumbling (for the most part unintelligibly) brief snatches of the lyrics which were projected onto a large screen at the front of the sanctuary. Even the younger members of the congregation often seemed distracted and confused, until we finally sang a traditional hymn — then *everyone* sang! Sadly tempo, volume, rhythm, and constant repetition of the contemporary praise songs was more appropriate for a dance or a pep rally, certainly not a worship service.

Do we understand what worship is? Do we understand the emotional state and frame of mind the music sung in worship is supposed to produce? Are we mistaking the aggressive energy being released through the triggering of the body's "fight-or-flight syndrome" today for an authentic spiritual "high"?

Have we lost our way and wandered into pagan practices that are not only contrary to our beliefs, but are potentially *dangerous?* Did King David dance wildly every Sabbath before the Ark of the Covenant? Did the Jews and later the early Christian church try to "turn everyone on" with aggressive worship music? Have we mistaken emotionalism for spiritual growth? Would Jesus Christ, our Lord and Savior, be honored by what we do to "turn ourselves on" for Him?

## My Background

I have an earned doctorate in both music and history. I have many books published, as well as CDs released. I have composed the musical scores to several feature films, plus many documentaries and commercials. I also served as minister of music in many churches, the most recent being Calvary Church in Santa Ana, California. This is the largest church in Orange County, California, and it has state-of-the-art equipment. I conducted and arranged music for a seventy-piece orchestra, a ninety-voice choir, plus many other musical units.

In addition, I have composed many original works for church choirs and orchestras, as well as several published contemporary praise songs. In addition, I am a regular clinician-lecturer for *Music California,* the largest annual gathering of Christian music ministers and directors, publishers, and Christian music artists in the United States, held annually in San Diego (always the week after Easter), which was developed and is directed by a close friend and fine Christian musician, O. D. Hall.

Quite often I'm brought in as a consultant or clinician for

churches or church music organizations on how to develop a *blended* church music program, one that integrates contemporary Christian praise songs with hymns, spirituals, and major choral works. Toward the end of this book you will find a list of "Do's and Don'ts" regarding the integration of contemporary music with a traditional program.

Several years ago I was asked, with other leading specialists in American music, to help the Coca-Cola Corporation develop a music appreciation course for junior high students.

My book *All That Jazz: A History of Afro-American Music* is published by Scarecrow Press, and is available through the Internet on *amazon.com*. Recently I was asked to write an important part for a new book to be released in December 2000, *The Instrumental Resource Book for Church and School Music Directors,* published by LifeWay Christian Resources in Nashville, Tennessee.

While on the faculty of the University of Southern California, I lectured and taught courses in film scoring, arranging and composition, improvisation, keyboard styles, and two popular large lecture classes, *The History of Jazz* and *American Folk, Pop and Rock* (a survey of indigenous American music from our beginnings to today).

My father was a professional musician and bandleader in Denver, Colorado. Both of my sons, Dana and David, are musicians. Dana is a professor of music at Orange Coast College, and David is a businessman who writes and plays contemporary pop music. As I learned from my father, my sons have learned from me. However, I also have learned a great deal from my sons regarding the revolution in pop music that took place in America beginning in the 1950s.

### Rock 'n Roll

A new style of music, originally called *rock 'n roll* (suggesting the motion made while having sexual intercourse, according to Bo Diddley who is credited with first using the phrase, then picked up by a Cleveland disc jockey by the name of Allen Fried) and applied to this emerging *white* version of what was previously called *rhythm 'n blues* — a style of Afro-American music that grew out of the classic blues styles, but with a rhythm section added so the music would be more danceable.

Black leaders of this music included *Bo Diddley, Little Richard, James Brown* and *B. B. King.* White "cover" groups grew out of this style of music and became widely prominent, including, *Bill Haley and the Comets, Richie Valens, Buddy Holly and Jim Croce.*

Then, out of Memphis, a former truck driver turned rhythm 'n blues singer shot to the front of the pack, thanks largely to the clever management by Colonel Tom Parker. Elvis Presley was at the right place at the right time. Television was becoming increasingly common in American homes, FM radio was introduced, and the discretionary income available to teenagers reached an all-time high, causing record companies to abandon traditional American "pop" and swing music for this "new" music called rock 'n roll. How lucrative was it? It is estimated that Elvis earned over two hundred million dollars in his relatively short career. His estate, including the shrine to Elvis (Graceland Mansion) has earned over two billion dollars since his death.

## What Is It?

Rock 'n roll is basically Afro-American rhythm 'n blues, with some country-western musical overtones. The basic message is simple: sex is good, life is fun, come to the party and dance, dance, dance. Dick Clark jumped on the bandwagon with his weekly television show "American Bandstand," which featured these new artists, live or recorded, with acres of teenagers wiggling sensuously to the music.

As a result of this newly-discovered mother lode, record

sales in America rose from slightly over five hundred million dollars annually in the early 1950s to close to twenty billion dollars today. When Clive Davis, a visionary recording industry guru, took over the pop recording department for RCA Records, the company was grossing around thirty million dollars a year. When he left, they were grossing over three hundred million dollars a year. Single albums, like Carol King's *Tapestry,* grossed over eighty-five million dollars. The Beatles *Abbey Road* album has grossed over one hundred million dollars, and is still selling today. Suddenly more money was to be made in the recording industry than in all the other entertainment industries combined, including motion pictures. This caused a major shift in the entertainment industry, one that is still reaping the profits from the introduction of rock 'n roll into the American vocabulary.

Voice of America and Voice of Asia, two armed services radio-broadcasting stations designed to not only entertain our troops overseas but also to sell the American dream through its music, continued to operate during the Cold War. Millions in Europe and Asia were soon hooked on American music and began buying records as fast as they could be exported.

In the 1960s a new version of rock 'n roll developed. It was called *rock* music. Led by the invasion of young British groups like the *Beatles* and the *Rolling Stones,* this music became further removed from its Afro-American roots. The emphasis was primarily on drugs, sex, and rebellion. Although the Beatles were originally "cute," with their pageboy haircuts and Nehru jackets, they soon abandoned their "clean" format for a more "in-your-face," raunchy musical and physical style pioneered by the Rolling Stones.

The manager of the Rolling Stones told them early on that their *primary* musical and theatrical mission was to get under the skin of the parents of the teenagers with their sexually explicit lyrics, open endorsement of drugs, and anarchistic behavior and message. The music was openly anti-Christian, anti-establishment, and narcissistic with its constant emphasis on self-gratification. The music became louder, more raucous, and moved totally away from any other previous styles dictating good taste and artistic sensitivity. The battle cry was condensed into their simple motto: *"Sex, Drugs and Rock 'n Roll."*

## Jesus Movement

At the same time that the country seemed to be going to hell in a handbasket, a spiritual revival was also taking place. The Bible says that *when evil abounds, God will raise a standard.* There began to emerge several centers in the United States where young people, disappointed with the fruits of rock music and the drug- and sex-centered lifestyle, were beginning to turn to Christ.

On the West Coast, Chuck Smith in Costa Mesa, California, began working with burned-out hippies and former doped-up surfers to create the very effective and still-growing *Calvary Chapel,* which has churches all over the United States and even outside of our country. Their training program for young ministers is second to none, and their loyalty to teaching the Bible and nothing else has served them well.

This ministry decided to hang on to the basic format of rock 'n roll, spiritualize the lyrics, tone down the volume, and introduce strong American folk influences. Soon Calvary Chapel established their own FM station which broadcast this new type of Christian music across Southern California, as well as spiritual messages and teaching tapes. Out of this ministry has come some of the most moving, important, and worth-preserving contemporary praise songs of today. The emphasis on spiritual dignity and avoiding extreme rhythms, volume, or repetitive lyrics (for the most part) has been successful.

North of Costa Mesa, in the black section of Los Angeles, Andrae Crouch, the son of a local black preacher began writing and recording some amazing music. In this music, we have a blend of black gospel with some rock influences and well-produced Hollywood sounds that give another dimension to contemporary Christian music. Less simplistic and more sophisticated than rock, Andrae's big hits like *My Tribute* have gone on to become standard repertoire in most churches today.

Bill Gaither and his wife brought to Christian music the best influences from Southern folk music and country-western music. The worshipful but "down home" feeling to most of their songs has been another positive influence on Christian music today.

Carol Cymbala, wife of the pastor and director of the *Brooklyn Tabernacle Choir* has contributed some of the most original, sophisticated, and inspirational contemporary Christian music today. Full of a strong mixture of Afro-American, jazz, and Hollywood smoothness, her lyrics never suffer, nor is the music ever too repetitious or simplistic.

## Christian Record Industry

Contemporary Christian music is the fastest growing part of today's record industry. While many other musical styles are beginning to fade, CCM is growing by leaps and bounds. We are all glad about that. Not only are the lyrics "spiritual," but the melodies and the artists are often much more musical than contemporary pop. However, there are some dangers when Christian music begins to enter the world of *rap* and *heavy metal*. How much can we use a rebellious musical style to sell the Christian message? Only time will tell.

One of the arguments of this book is that a great deal of contemporary Christian music is okay for concerts, records, MTV, or AM-FM radio. However, a great deal of it is *not* suitable for leading worship. The music was never intended for that purpose. To try to make it "fit" to attract young people is a dangerous policy. More and more, music ministries are becoming theatrical and are focusing more on "entertainment" than worship. *The purpose of music in worship is to edify — not entertain.*

Once a church sells out and starts "entertaining" their congregation, they are on a spiritually slippery path downward. On more than one occasion, I have visited a church where they put on a terrific show, aimed mostly at the young. However, in most instances, a worshipful, prayerful mood is ignored for a more Hollywood "glamour" presentation. This cannot only have tremendous spiritually negative affects on the congregation, but it can also confuse and spiritually damage the presenters (singers, musicians, dancers, actors).

## Fallout

Many of the contemporary Christian music artists have suffered fractured marriages, lifestyles, and alcohol and drug addiction. Many of the top artists have had affairs while representing the Lord, or have turned their backs on spouses and wise spiritual counseling, often fighting strong tendencies to alcohol, drug, or food addiction. Others have moved further and further away from the gospel message as their secular popularity rose, until several no longer represent themselves as "Christian" musicians.

If these fellow brothers and sisters in Christ have fallen into sin, shouldn't we forgive them if they have repented? The biblical answer is a strong "yes." However, should we not encourage them to withdraw from the spotlight, the adulation, and the position of being one of the major influences on young Christians until they are well grounded and mature? Again, I believe the spiritual answer is a strong "yes."

## Spiritual Dimension

The Devil, our old adversary, is *always* attacking the church. He is either persecuting the church directly through surrogate political and military leaders (as we see today in the Sudan, Iran, and China) or he is trying to *compromise* and *confuse* the gospel message and the emphasis on Scripture in our churches. The Bible clearly predicts that there will be *two* types of Christian churches in the "latter days" — one that remains faithful to the gospel, and one that becomes "worldly" (Rev. 3) and "apostate" (1 Tim. 4).

> Thou hast been in Eden the garden of God, every precious stone was thy covering, the sardius, topaz, and the diamond, the beryl, the onyx, and the jasper, the sapphire, the emerald, and the carbuncle, and gold: the workmanship of thy tabrets and of thy pipes was prepared in thee in the day that thou wast created.
>
> —Ezekiel 28: 13

From what we know of him, Lucifer (who after the fall became Satan — see Isaiah 14; Ezekiel 28) originally had something to do with leading music and worship. Wouldn't he turn to this area of his expertise, if possible, to weaken, confuse, or compromise the gospel? You bet he would! How he would like to (a) pervert and compromise our worship and (b) slyly shift the worship to him!

## Revolution

Rock 'n roll, and later rock music, brought about the single greatest revolution in popular musical styles in the past century. However, the foundation of their music was built upon sexual titillation, rebellion, and the embracing of drugs and the occult. Many of the musical styles championed by rock music came out of an occult background. Can we jettison the original lyrics and hang on to the original instrumental styles to better "sell" the Christian message to our young people? Not without prayerful and careful discernment as to just how far we will go in letting the world into the church instead of taking the church into the world.

Personally, I have found most teenagers turned off by the poor musical presentations of "their" music in churches, rather than turned on. Many people today are trying to *escape* the world, to find a place with peace, love, serenity, and dignity. Where better to go than the church. When they walk in looking for those attributes, and instead are hit in the eyes and ears with a poorly rehearsed imitative rock concert (with "Christian" lyrics) they often walk right back out again, terribly disillusioned.

## Summary

The church used to be a sanctuary; a place where you could escape the franticness, the torment, the sensuality of the world. Sadly, in many churches today, that is no longer the case. Has the world taken over the church? Have we sold our musical heritage to commercial interests more interested in making a profit than in saving souls? Have we carelessly and heartlessly dumped over three hundred years of sacred music in the ash-can of history, substituting simplistic, often childish, and in many instances scripturally unsound lyrics for the sake of reaching the lost? Have we unknowingly introduced into the sanctuary pagan rhythms, repetitive chanting, and loud emotional performances that are more apt to encourage demonic forces rather than drive them out, the original and primary purpose of worship before the sermon?

> By the rivers of Babylon, there we sat down, yea, we wept, when we remembered Zion. We hanged our harps upon the willows in the midst thereof. For there they that carried us away captive required of us a song; and they that wasted us required of us mirth, saying, Sing us one of the songs of Zion.
>
> —Psalm 137:1–3

# Rock Music and the Fight-or-Flight Syndrome

## Introduction

The human body is extremely sensitive to music. Music not only affects our emotional state, but it can affect the major organs and systems within our bodies. The vibrations produced when playing music pass *through* the body and impact every internal organ and system in some way. We not only *hear* music, but we *feel* it as well. Many contemporary rock fans no longer *listen* to the music; they let their bodies *feel* it instead.

## Vibration

Music is vibration. Vibration penetrates matter. When the jet airplane was first introduced to commercial travel, ground crews often suffered extreme forms of internal disorders, particularly those who flagged the planes into parking areas and were exposed to the high-pitched whine of the jet engines. After much research, it was discovered that the combination of the volume and the particular pitch frequencies of the engines were having negative effects on the internal organs of the bodies of the exposed ground crews. Today, those crews wear ear-protectors, as well as specially woven jumpsuits that contain a crossweave pattern and decibal absorption material to both break up the waves before they penetrate the body as well as to muffle them.

## The Dangers of Low Frequencies

Low frequency vibrations (bass and drums) are particularly hard to screen out and can cause extensive damage to the human body and mind if they are not monitored and kept below a ninety-decibal level. Several years ago, a scientist doing research on the effects of low-frequency soundwaves on the human body built a replica of the standard referee's whistle. When a referee in a sporting match blows his whistle, the air causes a cork ball to tumble around while the soundwaves pour over it, causing that penetrating, sharp sound. The scientist's replica was over six feet tall and the cork ball was almost twelve inches in diameter.

This particular scientist hooked up the whistle to a compressed air machine and decided to stay in the testing laboratory while his assistant turned on the air compressor, which caused the whistle to blow. The powerful low-frequencies — intensified by the cork ball — and the decibal level of the sound killed the scientist instantly. A follow-up autopsy revealed that the unfortunate scientist's internal organs had literally been "scrambled" by the power of the soundwaves.

## Plants, Animals and Music

Iowa State University has experimented with sound in relation to plants. For instance, they have discovered that playing soft, classical music over growing corn fields stimulates both yield and growth time. Similar posititve results have occured when playing pleasant, light classical music in the barns when cows are milked and in the hen house when chickens are laying eggs.

A recent experiment of playing different styles of music at

different decibal levels over identical trays of pansy flowers also revealed startling results. The flowers responded positively to light classical and acoustic jazz. However, the trays over which hard rock music was played — that's another story. Those flowers withered and died within hours.

## Seven-Eleven Gang Control

Recently the Seven-Eleven convenience store chain was having increasing problems in major metropolitan areas with gangs hanging around their stores. They found that playing light classical music — Mozart, Bach, Beethoven, etc. — over loudspeakers in and outside the store caused the gangs to leave. Why? Some have postulated that these gangs use contemporary rap and hard rock music to stimulate their aggressive tendencies, while classical music weakens and dissipates them. It's just a theory, but the idea works.

## Fight-or-Flight Syndrome

Scientists have confirmed that we all possess an ancient protective device called the "fight-or-flight" syndrome. Sudden, sharp loud noises represents "danger" to our instinctual and protective subconscious mind. The brain responds immediately, sending signals to the endocrine gland system and other parts of the body that will give the body a sudden burst of aggressive energy that can be used to (a) fight off a surprise attack or (b) escape by having enough additional energy to run or climb out of danger.

The glands that are most responsible for producing this emergency burst of aggressive energy are the adrenal glands, two small pear-shaped organs that sit one atop each kidney. They produce an enzyme called *adrenaline,* which gives the body more energy and strength, and the mind more power to overcome fear with aggression. They are part of a larger system called the endocrine gland system which includes our (a) testicles or ovaries, (b) the adrenal glands, (c) the thalamus gland, (d) the thyroid gland, (e) the pituitary gland, and (f) the pineal gland — all of which have powerful effects, positive and negative, on the human body.

The discovery and understanding of the endocrine gland system was one of the later discoveries of modern medicine. It wasn't until the late nineteenth century that this system and its affects on the human body was discovered. Even today, the gonads (testes, ovaries), adrenal glands, thalamus, thyroid, pituitary, and pineal glands are still somewhat mysterious in our total understanding of their purpose and affects on the body and the mind.

Surprisingly, Hindu Yogis were well aware of the endocrine gland system and its effects on the body and mind before modern medicine. Many of their exercises are designed to stimulate or modify one or more of these mysterious glands. The Hindus were also the first culture to realize both the healing as well as the damaging potential of music. Today, the classical music of northern India carefully organizes itself around a specific vocabulary of scales and rhythms called "ragas." These ragas are specifically for (a) morning, afternoon, or evening, (b) spring, summer, fall, or winter, or (c) romance, celebration, war preparation, etc. Indian musicians respect the power of music and will not abuse it by playing the wrong type of music at the wrong time, or for a function for which it is not suited.

Mankind soon learned how to artificially stimulate the adrenal glands by using primarily percussive and low-pitched instruments, playing aggressive-sounding and repetitive rhythms. To Native Americans, dancing around the campfire doing a war dance before going into battle was an important part of their preparation for combat. The rhythms, the dancing, the aggressive shouting and singing — all were designed to overcome personal fears of death and to activate their aggressive nature as well as give them "supernatural" strength.

As late as the American Civil War, infantry units went into battle with drummers — unknowingly stimulating their adrenal glands, giving them additional energy and aggressiveness. The youngest casualty in the American Civil War was a twelve-year-old drummer for the North, killed in the Battle of Vicksburg.

The development in our last century of sophisticated music amplification gear, and recording and playback systems has allowed the creation of an aggressive style of modern music called "rock" that activates the aggressiveness and increased energy levels in the listener as a result of their subconscious reaction to loud, percussive sounds, booming basses, and shouted lyrics.

The frantic, aggressive, orgiastic, almost uncontrollable energy level released at a typical rock concert is often mistaken by the audience and the performers alike as a demonstration of musical artistic ability. Actually, the level of artistic expression is secondary to their ability to stimulate audience reaction through triggering the fight-or-flight syndrome. The repetitive, constant loud backbeat of the rock drummer, the pulsating (at an ear-splitting level), low-frequency vibrations, and the soaring, wailing, crying sounds of the amplified guitar trigger major subconscious emotional responses in the body, primarily stimulating aggressiveness, as well as providing increasing, but difficult to control, energy.

The frenzied reactions in the audience often result in violence of some kind, both during and after the concert. It is very difficult to get insurance in most performance venues for a rock concert. There have been too many riots, fights, murders, assaults, rapes, and out-of-control audiences. Only the supergroups can afford the insurance and the added security for a rock concert. Even then, events can get out of control.

Shortly after rock 'n roll became rock music, the Beatles, a British group out of Liverpool, England, handled brilliantly by their new manager Brian Epstein (who died of a drug over-dose in his own swimming pool) became the first "supergroup" of rock music and the first major British import of what had been primarily, until then, an Afro-American musical style. Although the songwriting partnership of Paul McCartney and John Lennon produced some lovely songs that have become standards, their primary affect on audiences was triggered by the more aggressive and loud rock tunes that they also per-formed.

Following close behind the Beatles were the Rolling Stones, another British group. The Stones began as a copy of the more polite Beatles. However, they soon abandoned that style, set-tling for a raunchy, loud, offensive, aggressive style of music that even to this day nets them over eighty million dollars whenever they decide to tour the United States.

Their manager told them, when they changed styles early on, that their primary purpose was to a) alienate parents with their music, b) speak to the normal rebellious nature of the typical teenager, and c) drive their audiences into a frenzy with the loudest and most aggressive music ever recorded and per-formed up to that point.

## Music Has Nothing to Do With It

Ask *any* fan of the Rolling Stones, Michael Jackson, Kiss, or any other rock group, to sing at least eight measures of any hit song that these groups have recorded. They can't, not only because the "music" itself contains so little content, but also because they are fans for different reasons. Their favorite groups give them the biggest *rush,* the lyrics to their songs are the most provocative, and they are drawn to their theatri-cal presentations in concert.

In most instances in the groups named above plus hun-dreds more, the essential historical elements defining a musi-cal composition are *not* present — form, melody, harmony, and a coherent, inoffensive, and logical lyric.

Hard rock is not music; it is amplified noise, with offensive lyrics that are shouted and screamed through a PA system at ear–splitting levels, over a repetitive bass line and simplistic chord structure. The essence of hard rock is in the presentation — volume, emotional rage, offensive or obscene lyrics, and very visible and suggestive body movements by the "artists" while they are performing.

Whether they know it or not, the primary power and draw of this style of music is in their ability to "turn on" the listener by triggering their fight-or-flight syndrome. Once triggered, the body is actually getting "high" on its own internally–produced drug, resulting in a heightened sense of awareness, an increase in body energy, and an increased tendency to aggressive and anti-social behavior.

Woodstock, the most remarkable rock concert of the sixties, set a new standard of borderline anarchy by an audience of thousands. At the recent thirtieth anniversary of this concert, the audience got totally out of control. The music had become more aggressive and louder, and as a result the promoters ended up with an out-of-control mob that eventually caused hundreds of thousands of dollars of damage to cars, tents, neighboring property, and other facilities, as well as many reported (and unreported) rapes, drug overdoses, and unprovoked assaults.

There are very few large rock festivals today. The liability insurance to produce such an event is astronomical. The security costs are also severe. When they do occur, they are shorter, feature fewer groups, are more subdued, and very heavy security is involved. Even with these precautions, outbreaks of rage, rape, drug overdose, drunkeness, sexual exposure, and violence are common, but are quickly hushed up by the record companies and the promoters.

As a result, kids today seeking the *real* thrills of the past are often drawn to secret, underground rock concerts — performed by unknown but aggressive heavy metal rock groups in abandoned buildings and warehouses that can go on for hours. Many like to increase their aggressiveness by taking amphetimines and dancing in front of the stage in an area known as the "pit." Those who dance in the pit are allowed maximum expressions of violence. Anything goes in the "pit" from biting, kicking, slugging, self-flagellations, sexual exposure, gang-rape — you name it, it happens in the "pit." Hundreds of young adults, male and female, often pummel each other joyously as their hearing is being destroyed by the volume of the music blasting into their ears at close range. What's the trigger for this experience? Rock music.

## Rap

Rap is primarily an urban form of black poetry set to "music." It actually grew out of an African tradition of a tribal "griot," a poet who was allowed to make scatalogical remarks to anyone in the tribe, reveal embarrassing secrets, and make fun of anyone — including the chief. The "griot" in the African tribe was what the court jester was to the kings and queens of western Europe.

Rap reveals once and for all that "rock" music is not music. There is nothing musical about rap. It is aggressive, offensive, women-hating, police-hating, anarchistic thugs shouting their obscenities to a tribal repetitive rhythm. There is no melody, no form — only shouted (not sung) offensive lyrics and syncopated tribal rhythms over a repetitive bass line. Yet, "rap" records today rake in more money in record sales than that of classical and jazz music combined.

## Law Enforcement

Those caught up in these activities, along with some seriously misguided sociologists, psychologists, and youth apologists, claim that this kind of music and activity is a "healthy" outlet for normal pent-up teenage angst, and that it should be not only tolerated but encouraged. Some of this propaganda is coming from the record companies, who make billions of dollars from this junk.

Any police department of any city having to deal with the after effects of a rock concert or "rage" gathering will tell you a different story. In having to deal with the anger, frustration, and rage when brought in to restore law and order, they see these gatherings as a deliberately provocative challenge of the rules of public safety. They see these events as deliberately promoting teenage anger, sexual frustration, rage, and rebellion against all forms of authority — which usually results in dangerous outbreaks of violence, suicide, drug overdose, alcoholism, rape, assault, and even murder. Law enforcement wants these events banned, with heavy penalties for those producing the events.

## Music as a Drug

One of the most dangerous drugs on the market today is rock music. The overstimulation of the endocrine glands, as well as other deleterious changes in the body and often the accompanying ingestion of illegal substances, has wreaked havoc in our culture. The increasing incidents of outbreaks of teenage violence — from Columbine High School in Ingelwood, Colorado, to the murder of a teenager at the Altamont Rock Festival in Oakland, California years ago — have one thing in common: rock music.

Rock music has moved indoors, into the privacy of a teenagers room, where he or she can watch random acts of violence, sex, anarchy, drug use, and social nihilism on the most popular youth channel on TV today: MTV. I challenge any reader who has not spent a few hours watching this channel to do so. You will be amazed at what you see and hear — all in the name of acceptable teenage entertainment. MTV, like CNN, is international. They are the two most popular and powerful television channels in the world.

The record companies have long delayed a necessary investigation into the uncontrolled use of some of their musical products; particularly for young adults. Why? Billions of dollars are at stake. The recording industry today is approximately a twenty billion dollar a year industry, of which more than seventy percent of the product is aimed at teenagers and pre-teens.

The recent popularity of "rap" and "grunge" music, with it's angry "let's get 'em" or "let's all commit suicide" (as Kurt Cobain, a leading grunge artist, did) have added another dimension to the molotov cocktail of social anarchy that threatens our society — in a more serious and dangerous way than any outside force could ever accomplish.

## Music-Led Anarchy

The combination of illegal drugs, loud aggressive music, permissive parents, occult-based television and movie themes, a godless education system, and lyrics of rock songs that call for "destruction" and hate, have produced some of the most horrific and difficult-to-understand crimes in modern history. We are moving toward controlling the drugs — but *what about the music?* The music lights the fuse that produces the explosion!

Without understanding how dangerous these forms of music are and without moves to control their distribution, the problem will not only still be there, but *will get worse.*

A morally-confused radical (even by rock standards) recording "artist" by the name of Marilyn Manson (he took his name from Marilyn Monroe and mass-killer and psychopath Charles Manson) has produced some of the most terrifying, horrific, and anarchistic music ever recorded. It is interesting that when investigators began to look at the lifestyles and musical tastes of several recent teenage murderers, the one thing they had in common was *they all listened to and adored Marilyn Manson.*

## Contemporary Christian Music

Sadly, the Christian music recording industry has gone the way of the rock world. In their annual award show (the Dove Awards) there was not a category of pop music from rock to rap that wasn't represented in Christian music categories. We not only have Christian "rap," we have Christian "grunge," "heavy-metal," and "hip-hop." As a result, Christian record sales are booming. Artists are posing for increasingly sexually provocative or socially anarchistic album covers. The socially rebellious look — everything from tattoos to nose and ear-rings — now appear in the pictures of supposedly "Christian" artists.

## Biblical Warning

Paul the apostle saw these times — through the power of the Holy Spirit — and warns us what to look for in such revealing passages as 2 Timothy 3:1–5:

> This know also, that in the last days perilous times shall come. For men shall be lovers of their own selves, covetous, boasters, proud, blasphemers, disobedient to parents, un-thankful, unholy, Without natural affection, trucebreakers, false accusers, incontinent, fierce, despisers of those that are good, Traitors, heady, highminded, lovers of pleasures more than lovers of God; Having a form of godliness, but denying the power thereof: from such turn away.

## Fox in the Chicken-Coop

Sadly, we have let the wily fox, Satan, into our sanctuaries in our desparate efforts to attract teenagers and worldly adults to our worship services. Rather than lifting the name of our Lord with dignity and honor, we are debasing everything He stands for. We rationalize all this with the statement, "Things are different today!" Are they? Take time to read First and Second Corinthians. You will find that things are not that much different.

## Cause and Effect

Loud repetitive music, with a heavy percussion beat on two and four, along with a pulsating low-frequency bass, accompanied by screaming guitars and lyrics shouting blasphemies and obscenities that call for acts of violence are a *common thread* connecting most recent outbreaks of teenage violence.

Legislators can move to take away our guns, crack down on dope, and increase the prison sentences for teenage offenders, but until society identifies and deals with the *root cause* of most of this — the music — we haven't even begun to solve the problem. We are in a cultural civil war that may bring down our civilization, yet most adults today are either not aware of it or choose to ignore it.

Emotionally-disturbed children and adults, flooding their brains with musical anarchy and violence, are time bombs waiting to go off. The constant bombarding of these same damaged psyches with visions of violence presented as "entertainment" by greedy and unthoughtful recording, film, and television producers, has made many adults today fearful of their own teenage children.

This is *not* a problem about censorship. It *is* a problem about social and moral responsibility. We may have to mount large class-action suits against the entertainment industry, as we have done with the tobacco industry for the damage they have caused. A few decades ago our society saw the uncontrolled promotion, glamorization, and use of alcohol and tobacco as an individual's responsibility. Today we see the uncontrolled promotion and use of these substances as a serious threat to *society itself.* May we also begin to see the same sense of social responsibility directed at the uncontrolled use of music as a drug in our culture.

## Summary

As shocking as these discoveries are, it is even more shocking to see this music being welcomed with open arms into the sanctuaries of our churches. Have we lost our minds?

Are we so divorced from understanding spiritual warfare that we cannot understand that Satan wants to undermine and compromise our worship? Have we so given in to society and our teen-agers that we look the other way while evil slithers into our churches — all because we want to attract more teenagers and worldly non-believers?

Why would they want to come and stay with us when we present them with the same things they are running away from in our morally decadent society?

Does this mean that all contemporary praise music is bad? Certainly not! However, it does challenge us to use biblical standards in selecting and deciding what is and is not appropriate in that most sacred part of our religious service — the fervent worship of our Lord and Savior, Jesus Christ.

# The Bible and Music

Praise ye the LORD: for it is good to sing praises unto our God; for it is pleasant; and praise is comely.

—Psalm 147:1

## Introduction

Music was an important means of personal and artistic expression in ancient biblical times. However, the topic of music does not play a large role in Scripture. The expression of music is usually defined in two categories: instrumental and vocal. We will examine the vocal musical references and then instrumental.

## Vocal Music

Praise ye the LORD. Sing unto the LORD a new song, and his praise in the congregation of saints.

—Psalm 149:1

Modern science has discovered that when something is "sung" rather than spoken, it is more likely to be remembered at a later time. It seems that our long-term memory is in the right hemisphere of the brain. This hemisphere is extremely sensitive to music. Tribal societies must have intuitively known this, for prior to the discovery of the alphabet and the writing down of important events, all historical, religious, and moral lessons were *sung*.

Early Jewish music was primarily vocal. The hand-held lyre, much like a smaller version of the harp, was the most common instrument used to accompany songs. The Bible's first reference to singing is in Genesis 31:27, where it was part of the ceremony preceding sending away visiting guests or traveling loved ones.

We have only vague references and inferences again until the triumphant *Song of Moses* (Exod. 15), which celebrates the parting of the Red Sea for the children of Israel and the drowning of Pharaoh's pursuing chariots. In the same chapter, we have Miriam's song, accompanied by the timbrel (tambourine) and dancing — again, celebrating Israel's deliverance from Pharaoh.

Two other *antiphonal* (leader-chorus) songs appear — one in Psalm 136 and the other in First Samuel 18:6–7. A work song, associated with the digging of a well (Beersheba) was described in Numbers 21:17–18.

Moses gave Israel his last warnings in the continuation of the *Song of Moses* in Deuteronomy 32:1–4. Deborah and Barak sang a triumphant song in Judges 5:1–31 celebrating Israel's victory of their enemies. David was received by song by Israel's women after his victory over Goliath (1 Sam. 19:35). The Old Testament lists singing among men and women as a distinct social pleasure in Second Samuel 19:35.

Solomon not only wrote hundreds of proverbs, he also wrote one thousand and five songs (1 Kings 4:32). Singing was common in ancient Israel. David's trained choir numbered two hundred eighty-eight. This choir was not only continued, but expanded in size under Solomon (2 Chron. 5:12). One of the most detailed and interesting descriptions of music in the Old Testament occurs in Second Chronicles 5 and 6, when Solomon dedicates the newly-built Temple in Jerusalem.

Even after the division of the kingdom, the kings of Judah not only continued the Temple choir, but continued to expand it. Even after the destruction of the Temple by the Babylonians and Babylonian captivity, righteous praise music was heard in Jerusalem and Israel (Ezra 2:41; 3:11; 7:24; and Nehemiah 7:44; 10:28). The "songs of Zion" were world-famous (Ps. 137:3).

The primary purpose of music in the Bible was to sing praises unto the Lord. The one hundred fifty Psalms were originally written as songs, and were meant to be sung. In an orthodox Jewish synagogue they are still sung today by the cantor or the choir. Between the fall *Feast of Trumpets* (Rosha Shahna) — which is also the Jewish New Year, and the following feast (fifteen days later) Yom Kippur, all one hundred fifty psalms are sung and recited in evening rituals in the synagogue.

David, the great warrior, poet, musician, and psalmist (song writer) left all of us with a wonderful legacy of spiritually inspired lyrics. Unfortunately, we do not have an accurate record of the ancient melodies to which these psalms were sung. We do know they were sung with great dignity, often accompanied by harp or other instruments.

## Instrumental Music

Musicians (players of a musical instrument) are mentioned in the recently discovered prism of Sennacherib (Assyrian king, 691 B.C.) as being part of the tribute that Judah gave to this powerful invading king. In Elisha's day, minstrels were common in Israel (2 Kings 3:15). The most commonly used instruments, outside of the lyre, were the timbrel (tambourine), associated string instruments, and trumpets, which were reserved for ceremonial announcements during the great holy days celebrated at the Temple.

## Modes or Scales

The nature of the modes or musical scales used are entirely speculative. However, there are two commonly used scales for traditional Hebrew folk music and synagogue chanting by the cantor. These two scales are the *Pentatonic* (CD-FGA-C) and the "Jewish" scale (C-Db-E-F-G-Ab-Bb-C). The *Arabic* scale (C-Db-E-F-G-Ab-B-C) and the Jewish scale are quite similar.

## New Testament

There are fewer references to music in the New Testament. Jesus warns His disciples in the Sermon on the Mount (Matt. 5–7) that when they pray, they are not to use "vain repetition, as the heathen do." Religious practices using music outside of Judaism and the early church were, for the most part, quite different. They commonly used *loud, repetitive, percussive and syncopated music, usually accompanied by hand-clapping, swaying, and dancing.* Singers would shout short, repetitive phrases over and over, and they used this style of music to put the worshippers into a trance-like state. This is the pagan style of "babbling" that Christ referred to in the Sermon on the Mount. It is common to most world religions and is gaining acceptance in the West through the New Age movement.

## Pagan Worship and Music in the Church

Are we beginning to "babble" in our worship services today, with the often seemingly never-ending repetitions of simplistic phrases? Have we deserted the biblical model for worship music, opting instead for a more emotional, exciting form of worship that is claimed to be more "spiritual"? *Are we getting "high" on the music instead of being authentically filled with the Holy Spirit?*

These are legitimate questions to ask in light of what we see happening on an increasing scale in the worship part of our church services today.

## Don't Be Unaware

Have we naively left open the door in our worship services for subtle satanic influences? We've already discussed that Lucifer, before he fell and became Satan, was *in charge of music and worship* (Isa. 14; Ezek. 28). Is he up to his old tricks in trying to pervert, distort, and confuse worshippers and lead them *away* from the one true Christ of the Bible to a more "modern" Christ, one more *suitable* for today's emotionally-driven, relativistic, "dumbed-down" society?

## Spiritual Guidelines

A good guideline for today's worship services on how they are to be practiced, how they are to be performed, and the selection of hymns and choruses should be (a) did Christ teach it? (b) was it taught or endorsed by the apostles in their writings, and (c) was it mentioned or commonly practiced by the early church?

> As I besought thee to abide still at Ephesus, when I went into Macedonia, that thou mightest charge some that they teach no other doctrine, Neither give heed to fables and endless genealogies, which minister questions, rather than godly edifying which is in faith: so do.
>
> —1 Timothy 1:3–4

From what we can gather through a careful examination of authentic historical documents, the early Christian church, prior to Christianity becoming a state religion and being sometimes amalgamated with other pagan religions and practices at the time in A.D. 312 under the Roman emperor Constantine, was very careful to avoid *any type* of pagan practice, whether in food, dress, ceremony or music. In other words, there is no biblical support for many of the worship and music practices being introduced to our contemporary churches. Are we sure we know what we're doing? Are we being obedient to Scripture and tradition?

> Now the Spirit speaketh expressly, that in the latter times some shall depart from the faith, giving heed to seducing spirits, and doctrines of devils; Speaking lies in hypocrisy; having their conscience seared with a hot iron.
>
> —1 Timothy 4:1–2

# Music and the Early Church

They are all gone aside, they are all together become filthy:
there is none that doeth good, no, not one.

—Psalm 14:3

## Introduction

The Christian church was born in A.D. 32, on the Jewish feast
of Pentecost, a feast that always occurred fifty days after Pass-
over. The original church and its beginnings are described carefully in the Book of Acts. Little is said regarding music during
their services. We can assume that the early church sang a
few familiar psalms, and then gradually introduced some contemporary hymns and praise songs. Songs were sung accappella. They were later accompanied by the harp (David's harp
— small, hand-held) and/or flute and timbrel (tambourine),
and later still, by some sort of lute or guitar.

## The Founding Church

From what we can determine, the early services were built
around (a) singing of a few songs, (b) the reading of a portion
of Scripture, (c) exegesis or a teaching on that scripture, (d)
prayer, (e) announcements and needs, followed by (f) communion and (g) fellowship.

Each church was taught from the first its direct dependence on the Holy Spirit and responsibility to Christ. Soon they became a center for propagating the Word of Life. Each church was independent of any organization or association of churches, yet intimate connection with other churches was maintained, a connection continually refreshed by frequent visits of brethren ministering the Word (Acts 15:36). The meetings being held in private houses, or in any rooms that could be obtained, or in the open air, no special buildings were required.

—*The Pilgrim Church,* E.H. Broadbent, p. 27

## The State Church

When the Roman emperor Constantine declared Christianity a "state" religion in A.D. 312, what was known as the "Christian" church suddenly became a mixture of pagan and Christian rituals. Pagan holidays were given names of early Christian "saints." Christ's birthday was said to have occurred, luckily for the early church, on Saturnalia, one of the biggest of the pagan Roman festivals that took place on December 25, complete with decorated trees, the exchange of presents, and the ceremony of the yule log.

The celebration of Christ's resurrection also received a pagan name, "Easter," a derivative of the name of an earlier Babylonian female goddess of fertility, "Ishtar." Many of the ceremonies, rituals, and other practices associated still to this day with the Eastern Orthodox or Roman Catholic Church had their origin in ancient Babylon.

## State Church Music

Lost are the small intimate congregations. Now large, lavishly decorated buildings house the worship of God. Stately processionals and recessionals, as well as music for other parts of the service are now led by a professional choir of trained priests or novitiates. Later, the accompaniment of the choral music was supplemented by the organ and the brass choir. Congregational participation was limited to a few responses, and an occasional short hymn.

Professional composers, beginning in the fourteenth century, began writing extended works based on the outline of the Mass for special holidays and celebrations. One of the greatest church composers of this period was Palestrina. The music became ornate, complex, and almost impossible to perform.

## The Reformation

The Reformation brought congregational singing back to the church and eliminated (in most instances) the paid professional choir. Religious zeal produced a wealth of new hymns, and later extended choral and orchestral works by Johann Sebastian Bach, George F. Handel and others.

## The United States

The several early "Great Awakenings" or revivals in America helped to introduce new hymns based on folk songs and black gospel music and spirituals. Protestant churches usually had an organist, a choir, some soloists, and occasionally a hired orchestra to help perform major works. The service offered several opportunities for congregational singing and special Sunday evening musical performances, and hymn-sings were something all were excited about.

## The Black Church

The black church in America has produced some of the greatest Christian music of the past two centuries. Spirituals, for the most part, were written and sung before the Civil War, hence the emphasis on freedom, Moses, and "goin' home." Post-Civil War witnessed the birth of early gospel music, simple folk-like melodies, often accompanied by guitar, harmonica, and homemade bass. These songs were lifted from the many storefront churches in New Orleans and later, urban centers in the north.

## Modern Gospel

Modern black gospel music began with Thomas A. Dorsey, a repentant black blues singer from Chicago who, after coming to find the Lord, made it his mission to introduce into black churches music that they could more strongly relate too. Interestingly enough, many of the large urban black churches had gone "white" in their music liturgy and resisted this attempt to bring back their own music into their own church. As we know, eventually this movement caught on, becoming the strongest influence on contemporary Protestant Christian music in America to this day.

## White Gospel

Throughout the South and on local radio stations, many country-western, folk-orientated white gospel groups appeared. This earthy, down home style caught on and is second only to black gospel as a major influence on contemporary Christian music. Bill Gaither, the well-known Christian songwriter, has championed this style, with his "down home" get-togethers of major artists on Christian television, radio, CDs, and concert tours.

## Urban Gospel

Another major influence on contemporary Christian music is urban gospel. Borrowing heavily from rhythm 'n blues, this style, as best demonstrated by such artists as Andrae Crouch and such choral groups as the Brooklyn Tabernacle Choir, bring still another musical style into the wide and diverse world of Christian music today.

## Heavy Rock and Heavy Metal

Christian groups like Petra have been called to go into the rock clubs and perform and sing Christian music before an unsaved audience. It is a wonderful outreach to young people, one that I believe is sincere, but it incorporates a style of music that may be a bridge between the rock-fan salvation but is the antitheses of everything worship music should be in the sanctuary.

## Christian Rap

Rap music is the rebirth of an ancient African tradition of the "griot," the tribal poet/social commentator. Looked upon in tribal Africa much like the court jester in Europe, the tribal griot had free reign to mock, reveal, or condemn anyone and everyone in the tribe for real or imaginary crimes and breaches of morality and etiquette. Rap music in America is sung by angry young urban blacks who see no way out, who champion violence, drugs, crime, cop-hating, women-hating, and general social anarchy. It is one of the most dangerous musical styles to come on the American scene. I can't see how it can transfer well to the message of salvation; however, there are Christian groups out there that are trying.

## Christian Folk Music

American folk music has always held a strong attraction for young audiences. Today, one often finds touring Christian musicians whose primary musical style is influenced by American folk — solo voices, accompanied by twelve-string guitar, sometimes flute or harmonica. This style of music is still a strong influence on contemporary Christian music.

## Urban Swing

There have been some attempts by well-known Christian arranger-composers like Ralph Carmichael to introduce into the musical mix a form of Christian music based on the musical styles of the great swing bands of the 1930s and 1940s. Often there are Christian singers who sound a lot like Frank Sinatra. Although exciting and usually musically well-presented, this is not a major influence today on Christian Music.

## Jazz

Again, there have been some attempts to produce jazz-orientated Christian CDs. The styles range from early Dixieland to late contemporary fusion. So far, the audiences are limited for this style of music that demands a lot from the listener.

## Urban Pop

Probably the strongest influences on recorded contemporary Christian music today comes from urban pop. The musical styles of everyone from Elvis Presley to Michael Jackson have rubbed off on some of the more high powered Christian CDs, using everything from Latin percussion to special electronic synthesizer sounds.

## Dove Awards

In looking over the lists of groups nominated for the Dove Awards in the various categories, I was struck that today there isn't a commercial style of American pop music that does not have its Christian equivalent. The good news is that if our teenagers are going to have to listen to this stuff, better it be with Christian artists and lyrics. The downside is, just how much "sanctification" can we get into Christian "salsa" (Latin) music? Most of these pop musical forms are based on dance-beats, often with sensuous rhythms and highly stimulating production effects. Have we gone past the point of no return? Are we weakening the message of the gospel by spreading it around in these faddish commercial styles?

## Summary

The church has lost its way today by allowing its music to be polluted to the degree that it has by commercial interests. Worship songs are not meant to be cute, promote finger-snapping, toe-tapping, and secret winks. Worship songs are meant to focus us for a few brief minutes out of our week on the Creator rather than the creature.

I am saddened to see so many worship services turned into spiritual pep rallies, with the flesh aroused rather than subdued, with the human pride pumped up rather than humbled. Are we sure God wants this kind of music in His sanctuary? If the answer is "yes," then what is the litmus test to get into worship?

> Concerning the works of men, by the word of thy lips I have kept me from the paths of the destroyer.
>
> —Psalm 17:4

# The Nuts and Bolts of Music

## The Lyric

For God is not the author of confusion, but of peace, as in all churches of the saints.

—1 Corinthians 14:33

A pastor friend of mine told me a humorous story that points out the differences between traditional hymns and many contemporary Christian praise songs in the lyric department. According to this story, a traditional lyric would describe a real situation in the following manner:

Martha! The cows have broken through the fence and are eating the corn!

Set to a contemporary lyric concept that same lyric might read:

Martha, oh Martha, my sweet and lovely Martha, the love,
the love of my life!
The cows, the cows the brown, black white and gray cows
have broken, have destroyed, have invaded
Our precious field of corn, our most precious field of corn, I
said precious field of corn —

What, I ask you what, what are you, what am I what are all
of us to do to really do, I mean do, not wait but do, not
pray but do . . . do,do, do!

The above is an extreme example of the difference between
normal, direct communication in a lyric and the kind of distorted bumper-sticker lyrics we often hear today in contemporary Christian music.

### *Writing Lyrics*

Trying to create a perfect lyric that matches up with the other
seven musical ingredients is *very difficult*. It's one of the reasons there are few truly "great" songs, secular or Christian.
When there is a perfect match, the impact of the song on the
listener is *very powerful*.

A great lyric must create in the mind of the listener a)
empathy, b) sympathy, and c) identity. The listener must be
able to "feel" and empathize with the lyric, feel sympathy for
what's happening, and be able to identify themselves with the
situation being described in the lyric.

Most songs are short stories. They introduce characters
into events and develop those events to a meaningful climax.
We all love a good story, but a story with holes in it is confus-
ing and we soon lose interest. Compared to most of the lyrics
of the standard great hymns and spirituals, most contemporary praise songs fall short. In fact, most are more like nursery rhymes than wonderful stories that lead us and inspire us
in faith.

Martin Luther's *A Mighty Fortress* leads us step-by-step
through the protection our Savior offers us when under spiritual attack:

A mighty fortress is our God, A bulwark never failing.
Our helper He, amid the flood of mortal ills prevailing.

For still our ancient foe [Satan] doeth seek to work us woe.
His craft and pow'r are great, and armed with cruel hate.
On earth is not his equal.

This first verse reminds Christians that a) God is our protector, b) He will never fail, c) He'll be there during hard times, d) that Satan is our enemy, and e) that his power is great.

Did we in our own strength confide, Our striving would be losing
Were not the right man on our side, the man of God's own choosing.
Dost ask who that may be? Christ Jesus, it is He
Lord Sabaoth [Lord of the Sabbath] His name, from age to age the same
And He must win the battle.

This verse continues the drama, heightens it, and reveals that the man of God's choosing was Jesus Christ, who is the same today, and that it is He who must win the battle, not ourselves.

And tho this world with devils filled, should threaten to undo us.
We will not fear, for God hath willed His truth to triumph through us.
The prince of darkness grim, We tremble not for him.
His rage we can endure, for lo, his doom is sure;
One little word shall fell him.

Again, we are reminded that our primary adversary is the Devil. Although he is powerful, we are not to fear. God will triumph through our trials. We are not to tremble at his rage or roar, knowing that his fate was sealed on the cross, and that the Word of God rightly spoken by a true believer will cause him to flee.

That word above all earthly powers. No thanks to them
   abideth.
The Spirit and the gifts are ours, through Him who with us
   sideth.
Let goods and kindred go, this mortal life also
The body they may kill, God's truth abideth still;
His kingdom is forever!

Who's word? *God's Word!* It's above, stronger than all worldly powers. It is still here, no thanks to the secular world. We are indwelt with the Holy Spirit and each of us has been given valuable and powerful spiritual gifts — through Jesus. Let go of material things and the world — even life itself — for even though the enemy might kill the body it cannot touch the soul or slow the purpose of God's Word. The final reminder: His kingdom is an eternal kingdom!

What a message! What a sermon-in-a-song, in fact a good preacher could preach a sermon off of every verse in this hymn. Also, the lyric does not insult our intelligence by writing down to us, as if we are all in grade school. This lyric introduced characters, drama, a build to a climax, and a positive resolution. A great story in song.

### Contemporary Praise Song Lyric

On the other hand, here is a typical contemporary praise song lyric. Yes, I know that some contemporary praise songs have beautiful, well-constructed, deeply spiritual lyrics. On the other hand, this example is typical of the narcissistic shallowness of many songs today:

Gee, I want to love you a lot — deep within my heart,
I really want to love You.
Oh, I want to know You, to feel your feelings, know your
   mind

Looking in your eyes stirs me up inside and makes me
Want to really, yes really learn to love you more.

This is a slightly disguised version of a contemporary praise song that has been recorded by practically every major Christian artist. I find it to be dull, repetitive, insulting (to Jesus), suggesting a closeness that is more sexual than spiritual. This song could be sung by any man to any woman, or vice versa, without altering one word!

There is nothing in this lyric to suggest that it is a song to be sung in honor of the love we feel for Jesus Christ. In fact, it's embarrassing, sophomoric self-centeredness is more typical of a song or poem you would expect from a young high school student in love with a classmate. There is no scripture, no scriptural lesson, no ideas on how to get to love God more or *why* we should even try. Yet, this is a paraphrase of a very popular contemporary praise song. How about:

Our God, is a heavy dude, He reigns from heaven and is
    never rude
This dude rules with love, knowledge and power, every hour.
Our God is a heavy dude, He comes from above with lots of
    love.
Oh God, is a very heavy dude!

Another paraphrase of a very popular contemporary Christian lyric. You could be of almost any religious persuasion and sing this song with conviction, be you Buddhist, Muslim, or even Hindu. What makes Him *our God?* What right do we have to call Him *our God?* We'll never know, because the lyric doesn't tell us.

### Exceptions
Does this mean that all Christian songs must tell a lengthy, profound story or a complicated message of redemption? The

answer is *no*. Try on "Amazing Grace," or "Just As I Am,"
"Holy, Holy, Holy," or "Majesty." These songs are simple, but
at the same time *profound*.

## A Warning
In the book of Jeremiah, God tells His prophet how angry it
makes Him when those who claim to know Him and worship
Him approach Him in such a careless, irreverent manner. According to Jeremiah it makes God *furious*. Today's "God is my
buddy" songs go too far and infringe on the mighty power and
awesome nobility of the Creator of the universe.

## Summary
Pastors, music directors, members of the congregation: examine the lyrics of your praise songs. If they contain false doctrine, are patronizing to God, or insult your intelligence, *refuse
to sing them.* For some reason, congregations are terribly in-
timidated about speaking up regarding their spiritual and
musical frustrations in this area. Speak up! God will more likely
condemn you for *not* speaking up than for being bold.

> Now when they saw the boldness of Peter and John, and
> perceived that they were unlearned and ignorant men, they
> marvelled; and they took knowledge of them, that they had
> been with Jesus.
>
> —Acts 4:13

## Rhythm
And Moses turned, and went down from the mount, and the
two tables of the testimony were in his hand: the tables were
written on both their sides; on the one side and on the other
were they written. And the tables were the work of God,
and the writing was the writing of God, graven upon the
tables. And when Joshua heard the noise of the people as

they shouted, he said unto Moses, There is a noise of war in the camp. And he said, It is not the voice of them that shout for mastery, neither is it the voice of them that cry for being overcome: but the noise of them that sing do I hear. And it came to pass, as soon as he came nigh unto the camp, that he saw the calf, and the dancing: and Moses' anger waxed hot, and he cast the tables out of his hands, and brake them beneath the mount.

—Exodus 32:15–19

Dancing wildly to drums, singing repetitious pagan songs, worshipping the idol — sounds like an early version of "sex, drugs, and rock 'n roll," the battle cry of the hippie 1960s and the philosophical *essence* upon which contemporary rock music is built, Christian or non-Christian.

We will discover in this chapter that rhythm is the most powerful and dangerous part of music. For unknown spiritual reasons, certain rhythms will instantly attract demonic forces, trigger aggressive behavior, and destroy moral codes and any sense of modesty or self-control. Rhythm is not evil, but it is dangerous, and no amount of pasting religious lyrics above its rhythms can deny its deep and dangerous effects on the human body, mind, and spirit.

### What Is Music Made Of?

Music has seven basic ingredients: 1) rhythm, 2) form, 3) melody, 4) countermelody, 5) harmony, 6) texture (range and tone quality), and 7) style (dynamics, tempo, articulation). In this section we will examine rhythm. In subsequent sections we will deal with the other six important aspects of music.

### DNA

Just like a car engine (carburetor, distributor, etc.) any piece of music can be taken apart, and each part can be studied and analyzed. In fact, it is the subtle changes in one or more of these seven parts that produces new styles of music, and like a set of fingerprints, can identify the composer. A detailed analysis of these seven ingredients are the DNA of a musical style or composer. Knowing a musical style or composer's "DNA," a trained musician can duplicate or clone that style of music.

A few years ago I was active as a film composer in Hollywood. I had the opportunity to do the musical score for several major studio feature films. Most of these assignments were done under extreme time constraints. It seems that the producers always wait until the last minute for the music. Not only was I to compose original music for the film, often I needed to write appropriate music for a particular scene. For instance, in one film I had to produce an Italian version of pop "disco" style blaring from a radio somewhere in Rome.

I ran down to Tower Records on Sunset Boulevard, asked for their international section, and found some Italian disco. Breaking this style into the seven parts and analyzing the basic ingredients allowed me to write an "original" Italian disco piece for the film that sounded authentic.

As a result of understanding how to use this analysis technique, one can compose or arrange a piece of music in any musical style, historical or personal. A few years later I had the opportunity to underscore a television commercial for a new toy, one that required "rap" and techno-pop styles, as well as knowledge on how to use special electronic effects. In each instance, the most important characteristic of each style was the rhythm patterns.

### The Human Body

The first and most important ingredient in music is rhythm. The human body is rhythmic. We breathe rhythmically; our heart beats rhythmically (boom . . . boom, boom, etc.); all our involuntary systems function rhythmically. We walk and talk rhythmically. In fact when the drums "talk" in Africa, they are imitating the rhythm of speech. Natives at a distance can understand what's being said based on the rhythm alone.

We are much more sensitive to rhythm than to any other aspect of music. Our respiratory and circulatory systems as well as brainwaves and endocrine gland secretions are strongly influenced by rhythm. Our bodies literally try to "tune" themselves to rhythm. That's why years ago in boot camp in the military services they awakened the troops with the sounds of military marches, recorded or live.

A military march beat is approximately one hundred twenty-four beats per minute. When we awaken, our pulse rate is somewhere around seventy-three to seventy-eight beats per minute. The brain tries to speed up our pulse rate to where it more closely matches that of the music. The result: we wake up faster!

### Rhythm and the Spirits

Demonic forces seem to be very sensitive to rhythms. In cultures as diverse as Tibet and tribal Africa, we find sorcerers calling up demonic forces using repetitive and specific rhythms as a primary technique. Even today, occult religions of Latin America (performed in the United States as well) like *Santaria* (Cuba), *Macumba* (Brazil), and *Voodoo* (Haiti) all use drum rhythms to call forth the spirits.

In these ceremonies, these rhythms are repeated over and over while many dance in a frantic, careless manner. Then some members of the congregation (usually women) are eventually "possessed" by one of these spirits and they start speaking in an unknown tongue or in an unusual manner.

Once this happens, others gather around this person, often presenting gifts, and asking for personal advice from the demonic force that has possessed this person. Sometimes alcohol or hallucinogenic drugs are used. It is not uncommon for animal and in rare cases, human sacrifice to be involved. Mickey Hart, drummer for the rock group *The Grateful Dead,* has researched this in both Africa and Latin America. He has some amazing video footage of this process occurring. In every instance the *rhythm* of the drums triggered the arrival of the spirits. Years ago, a European-made film, *Black Orpheus* was filmed in and around Rio de Janeiro during "Carnival." One scene actually shows this ritual, and records the spirit voice speaking through one who is possessed.

Centers for this activity in our country are Miami, New Orleans, New York, and Los Angeles. If you doubt the authenticity of this statement, call the police departments of any of these cities and you will get an earful regarding their problems dealing with the fallout from these occult religious practices. In these cult religions, the master drummer is the most important person in the group. No drums, no worship!

### The Early Church
It is no accident that early church music lacked the highly syncopated and repetitive occult-inspired rhythms we hear sneaking into contemporary Christian music today. Early church fathers were well aware of the dangers of these syncopated, repetitive rhythms and made sure they did not infiltrate the music of the church. The early church was well aware of the dangers of certain syncopated patterns repeated over and over, and were severe in their restricting these rhythms to the world and pagan ceremonies.

In fact, suspicion bordering on paranoia kept a lot of exciting rhythmic elements out of church music until the twentieth century because the church at that time would rather be safe than sorry. They had a strong respect for the subtleties and power of music, particularly rhythm. They also knew that Satan was always trying to enter the sanctuary, one way or another.

## Spirituals

It was not until the Afro-American spirituals began to become widely popular, along with ragtime, jazz, and other forms of Afro-influenced music that we began to see some of these more syncopated, African-originated rhythms enter our contemporary church music and our churches. The composers and performers of these spirituals, and later gospel music, were very aware of which rhythms were dangerous for Christian worship.

The Afro-American churches of America today are actually a lot more sensitive to what rhythms are dangerous and which ones are not than the primarily "white" churches. Black churches, for the most part, are careful to keep out "dangerous" rhythms from their vibrant and heartfelt celebrations and worship services. They know, and will quickly identify, certain beat patterns as being "of the devil." The founder of modern gospel music in America, Thomas A. Dorsey, began his career as a blues singer by the name of "Tampa Red." When he found the Lord, he renounced his blues career and began writing, performing, and arranging Christian songs. His life and career were caught on camera for television in a film called *Say Amen Somebody!* That film is available for rent in many of the larger video rental outlets.

## Rock Music

The birth of rock 'n roll ('50s) and later rock music ('60s–present) allowed for and even invited in many of these demonically-inspired rhythm patterns. Many of the more popular early rock groups, like the Beatles, sought out "inspiration" from occult influenced religions like Hinduism, Native American music, and the music of Africa, the Middle East and Tibet. The battle cry of "sex, drugs, and rock 'n roll" was nothing new. Actually these moral excesses were the foundation of many of the primitive religions actually being practiced before and during the time of Christ and the early years of the church. Above everything else, rock music was meant to be loud, repetitious, carnal, and extremely suggestive sexually. It is a dangerous mistake to think that you can take the rock format, add Christian lyrics, and everything will be okay. The body will be getting the sensual message of the music, the mind will trigger the fight-or-flight syndrome stimulating aggressiveness and increased energy, but the spirit will be receiving a watered-down, simplistic "spiritual" message. Which one of the two messages do you think the listener will be most influenced by? You got it — the body, then the mind, and then the spirit. Isn't that a dangerous way to package the gospel of grace to a sick and unsaved world?

Worldwide popularity and tremendous access to the minds of our young people through AM and FM radio, records and CDs, live concerts, and the now all-pervasive MTV have allowed sex-crazed perverts, high on drugs, to introduce demonic rhythms calling forth dark forces to invade the minds of our youth. Shouldn't we be on our guard to protect our young Christians from some of these evil influences instead of co-opting them for the church because someone said the "kids" like it? Kids like violence, too. Should we begin using dramatized violence to sell Christ? Where do we stop?

The record industry today is a twenty billion dollar a year business, with most of the market (over sixty percent) devoted to influencing the minds of our young people. In the recent rash of violence on school campuses, the one constant thread that runs through each case is the fact that those accused of committing these horrible acts of violence were *all* deeply involved in some of the most violence-prone, demonically inspired music ever produced.

Now we have "Christian" rap! Rap is anger, violence, disrespect, and rebellion. How do you clean it up and sell it with a Christian message?

Imagine this scene: A parent enters their teenage boy's room and finds a pornographic magazine. When confronted, the boy says, "Gee mom, it's not regular pornography, it's Christian pornography! All of those girls are apologizing and asking forgiveness for exposing their nakedness. Me and my friends are praying for 'em!"

As a parent, would you buy that? I hope not. Then why are you buying Christian "rap" records when they appear in your child's room? What are we doing to the image of Christ when we try to market and package His message this way?

It's taken years for America to wake up and realize that smoking cigarettes eventually kills every third person who smokes. How did we allow this to happen for so many years? I believe that we are just beginning to wake up to the dangers of contemporary pop music, not only to our child's hearing (twenty-eight percent of all urban teenagers today have some form of hearing loss), but to their bodies, their minds and their spirits as well. Some day, when we wake up to the damage the uncontrolled record industry has done to our children and grandchildren, new laws will put them out of business. In the meantime, they operate with relative impunity, dropping suicide, violence, sexual perversion, and anarchy into the minds of our youth. The least we can do is keep it out of the church!

> The power is in the music. You've got to invite the adulation and the adrenaline. You've got to pull the adrenaline out of the audience and into you to feed on it — this is another chemical [drug] reaction. It's a crossfire of adrenaline while on stage. The minute you start, the audience gives you energy and you give it back.
>
> —Leading rock group guitarist

## Internal Destruction
The tobacco industry and the record industry, including MTV, in America are the most destructive internal social forces we

have ever faced. Just as we have begun to realize with the tobacco industry, hopefully (and soon) we will realize that we have allowed unscrupulous businessmen to cause more damage to our culture than an out-and-out military attack from a foreign invader. We have lost control of the shaping forces of home, church, and school that develop our future generation. We have turned over the reigns to these industries and we are reaping the harvest. By the way, the drug industry is a *byproduct* of the music industry. Directly or indirectly, the music business encourages the use of drugs, now the third largest industry in America.

### Demons in the Church
We have left the door open in our sanctuaries, evangelical rallies, and youth meetings to the evil forces of Satan through the tribal, demonically-inspired rhythms that have crept in from their recent introduction to rock music.

Does this mean that contemporary Christian music is demonically inspired? Certainly not! However, there is a certain naiveté on the part of contemporary Christian musicians, songwriters, arrangers, producers, and record companies regarding the potential dangers involved in "flirting" with these exciting, hypnotic, and dangerous beats.

### How Do We Recognize Dangerous Rhythms?
A simple test will help us recognize these dangerous rhythms. If it is (a) too loud, (b) too repetitive, and (c) highly syncopated, it is potentially dangerous. If you feel more like "moving, swaying, clapping" than listening to the lyrics, it is dangerous. If you find the music "turns you on," "hypes you up," makes you more emotional (not spiritual), it is dangerous. In other words, if you feel more like dancing than singing, you may be in trouble. If you are more conscious, not less, of members of the opposite sex as a result of the music, look out!

Remember, true worship is *lifting up* the name of Jesus. We should be *less* conscious of ourselves and more conscious of Him. We should feel that we have entered a heavenly atmosphere, not the local dance hall, bar, or strip club.

The early church was highly suspect of any rhythms that triggered strong physical responses, such as hand-clapping, toe-tapping, swaying, dancing, moving of the head up and down, etc. Early black churches would allow their parishioners to "dance" while under the power of the music and the Holy Spirit, but the dance was carefully restricted to lifting and putting down each foot. It was not allowed to cross one foot over the other or to move in any way that could be interpreted as sensuous. They knew the power of rhythm and defined its boundaries within their worship services, something many "white" Christian churches have yet to do.

The musical contributions from the Afro-American Church in America have certainly passed the test of being truly worshipful and Christ-centered. However, as we stated earlier, the black church is more aware of the dangers than the white church. In the white church's efforts to imitate the freedom and joy of worship often found in the black churches, they have often gone too far and have allowed demonically-inspired rhythms into the music.

Be particularly careful of African, Cuban, Latin, Indian, or Eastern rhythms. They are new (to our culture), they are exciting, but in most instances, *they don't belong in the church.*

Highly syncopated (off-beat accents) polyrhythms (more than one complicated rhythm being played at one time) are also dangerous. They trigger physical and emotional responses that are *contrary* to the tradition of worship within the church. Native pastors and missionaries in Africa, India, and parts of Latin America and Cuba are well aware of these dangers, and you *will not* find pagan rhythms in their worship songs.

Personally I have strong reservations about drums being used in worship services, unless they are performing a contemporary major work; a cantata, oratorio, or some sort of extended musical presentation where percussion is used to enhance and support the overall themes.

Black gospel relied on the Hammond B-3 organ, an electric bass, and often a tenor saxophone to give flavor to their music. Drum sets were not seen and used until recently in most black churches. Many still hesitate to add the drum set to their ensemble.

On the other hand, I have visited some predominately white churches where there was a drum set, a conga set (Cuban drums), and additional exotic percussion. In most instances, the drummers in these groups come out of the contemporary rock music world and are conditioned to play too loud and too repetitively. Many suffer some hearing loss and cannot play softly or blend with an ensemble.

### *Summary*

Be aware that rhythm is the most sensitive and the most powerful tool for demonic forces to invade church music. Be careful about tribal rhythms via Latin America, the Caribbean, Africa, Asia, or the Middle East, becoming the foundation for your praise songs. Remember that the early church was highly suspect of syncopated rhythms (for good reason) that suggested dance more than worship. Our Afro-American brothers and sisters in the church have brightened up worship with their joy and with their infectious rhythms — but be careful about going *beyond* their contributions to rhythmic worship.

Praise ye the LORD. Sing unto the LORD a new song, and his praise in the congregation of saints. Let Israel rejoice in him that made him: let the children of Zion be joyful in their King. Let them praise his name in the dance: let them sing praises unto him with the timbrel and harp. For the LORD taketh pleasure in his people: he will beautify the meek with salvation.

—Psalm 149:1–4

## Form

Ye also, as lively stones, are built up a spiritual house, an holy priesthood, to offer up spiritual sacrifices, acceptable to God by Jesus Christ.

—1 Peter 2:5

Very little music can be performed without form. Form is the organizing of music into contrasting phrases, sections, and movements. All great art is based on a careful balance between unity (predictability) and variety (spontaniety). Form is the architecture of music.

### *Simple Forms*

The most simple form is an ABA form:

A) "Praise the Lord, He's Risen Today" (4 measures)
B) "We are His children, we've come to sing" (4 measures) — different melody
A) "Praise the Lord, He's Risen Today (same as the first "A")

In this form, you have *unity* through the repetition of the "A" phrases and variety through the contrast of the "B" phrase, separating the two.

Other simple or common forms for songs include:

| | |
|---|---|
| ❖ AABA | ❖ABCD (rare) |
| ❖ ABCA | ❖ ABCC |
| ❖ ABBA | ❖ ABCB |

## Longer Works

The longer a piece of music, the more complex the form. Like building a building, a one-story cabin requires little knowledge of architecture. However, a twenty-story office building requires a great deal of knowledge in that area. The same is true for music. Longer forms in music include:

| | |
|---|---|
| ❖ Sonatas | ❖ Oratorios (such as "Messiah") |
| ❖ Concertos | ❖ Mass (Bach B Minor Mass) |
| ❖ Suites | ❖ Opera |
| ❖ Symphonies | ❖ Ballet |
| ❖ Light Opera | ❖ Overtures |
| ❖ Minuet | ❖ Marches |

Common forms used in writing the various movements of a sonata, concerto, or symphony include the a) sonata-allegro form, b) song form, c) rondo form, d) minuet and trio form, and a few others. It is not necessary for us to go into the internal structure of these movement forms since they are seldom used in a religious context, unless it is an oratorio, mass, or cantata.

One of the dissapointing aspects of a great deal of contemporary Christian music is its monotony. There seems to be much reluctance to seek more balance between unity and variety. Many works, from a form standpoint, are just plain monotonous. This shows a great lack of artistic sensitivity and a major departure from the hymns, spirituals, and extended church works of the past.

Music today is being used more and more to (a) modify an environment or (b) create a particular mood or feeling. Much of the New Age music of today, as well as Christian music, is *deliberately* monotonous and repetitive. Music no longer engages the intellectual side of the brain, the part that requires logic and balance, but instead concentrates on engaging the emotional side of the brain. The result is a temporary environment favoring a particular emotion achieved through constant, monotonous repetition. Some experts call this "right brain" music.

Although this type of music does create a mood and a temporary aural environment, it also tends to deaden or put to sleep the more cognitive parts of the brain where logic and meaning find their home. The danger here is that a person can be so lulled into an induced complacency through the repetitious music that they are *vulnerable* to illogical offerings from the pulpit.

This type of parishoner goes to church for the "rush," for the fun of being put into an altered state of consciousness in a safe environment. Stress, tension, and other negative feelings are reduced. However, the *desire* to examine the Word of God closely, to carefully monitor the doctrines being presented, like the complimented Bereans in the Book of Acts, disappears.

Once in this altered state of consciousness, the parishoner is vulnerable to false teaching. Pride-driven worship leaders are less suspicious or conscious of the fact that the Devil is *always* trying to attack the church, either through persecution from without or compromise and co-opting from within.

### What to Look For

If the music forms of the songs you are singing in church are too simplistic, constantly repetitious, and offer little balance between unity and variety, *question* their spiritual validity!

We are sometimes vulnerable here because (a) the "kids" like the music, (b) some people feel "good" after singing these monotonous songs, (c) these songs are very popular in the commercial market, and (d) the congregation is docile, blissed-out and seldom offers positive critiques to the pastor on his presentation.

In a bullfight, the matador wears the bull down through

monotonous passes, then he calls in the picadors to further weaken the bull through monotonous jabbings of the bull until the bull stands still — tired, confused, and unaware of what is going to happen to him when the matador finally approaches with the sword hidden in his cloak.

Many of the monotonous songs of today, often with scripturally and doctrinally questionable lyrics ("Jesus is my buddy, Jesus is my pal") are softening us up like the bull. Are we being deceived by satan?

> And saith unto him, All these things will I give thee, if thou wilt fall down and worship me.
> —Matthew 4:9

### Melody

> Thou that dwellest in the gardens, the companions hearken to thy voice: cause me to hear it.
> —Song of Solomon 8:13

Just as tribal societies and cultures, particularly those on or below the equator emphasized rhythm as the primary ingredient in their music, in the music of the northern hemisphere, i.e., Europe, Asia, the United States, and Canada, the emphasis is on melody.

What is melody? Melody is a musical tone that vibrates at a certain frequency as long as that tone is sustained or held. For instance, the note "A" on the piano, (the sixth white key up (right) from middle "C" (counting "C") is tuned to *A 440*. It is *the* note that orchestras and ensembles tune to. When struck, this piano key triggers a hammer which strikes a string which is tuned to vibrate at *four hundred and forty vibrations per second*. If we went an octave higher to the next "A," that note would vibrate at *eight hundred and eighty vibrations per second*.

As music goes higher, the rate of vibrations increase. As music goes lower, the rate of vibrations slow down. For instance the lowest "A" on the piano (bottom key on the left), vibrates at only *fifty-five vibrations per second.*

When one melody note changes to another, it either goes up or down. When it does, it creates what is called an "interval." These intervals are categorized as follows:

- *Perfect.* Intervals of the unison, octave, fifth, and fourth (four notes or five notes above or below the first note.
- *Consonant.* Intervals of the major and minor thirds and sixths.
- *Mild Dissonant.* Major second, minor seventh, and major ninth.
- *Dissonant.* Minor second, augmented fourth, major seventh, and minor ninth.
- *Compound.* Intervals larger than an octave (C to C - compound would be C to D above)

## Music and Emotion

Music is a language of emotion, and each element of music contributes to and reinforces a particular emotion being expressed. There are eight common emotional states (others are derivatives of one of these):

| | |
|---|---|
| - Mad | - Humorous, playful |
| - Sad | - Inspirational (ecological, patriotic, etc.) |
| - Glad | - Spiritual |
| - Sensual | - Romantic |

There are degrees of varying levels of intensity within each of these categories. Also, different cultures will express these emotions through music differently. Each interval creates an emotional feeling, no matter how temporary or fleeting. For instance:

❖ Perfect intervals create a feeling of openness, space, power (C-C, C-G, C-F)

❖ Consonant intervals are called "pretty" or "romantic" intervals (C-A [Ab], C-E [Eb])

❖ Mild dissonant intervals are dramatic  (C-D, C-Bb, C-D [ninth])

❖ Sharp dissonant intervals — pain, rage, sorrow, grief, tension (C-Db, C-F#, C-B, C-Db)

❖ Compound intervals suggest forward movement and high drama (greater than an octave)

### Mix and Match

A good composer will try to coordinate and match all seven elements of music in such a way that they are unified in sending a single emotional message at a time, unless there is a desire to create confusion and send a double signal.

### Intervals and Church Music

The Gregorian chants which were so much a part of the Catholic Church's musical liturgy from A.D. 900 to the Reformation in the sixteenth century are simple, unaccompanied, unison (no harmony) melodies built mostly around the perfect and consonant intervals. Even today, we turn to this style of music for a definitive sound typical of deep, reverent worship. The melodies are humbling, disarming, and gradually they will reduce stress in the listener. Sung in Latin, there was careful attention paid to vocal inflection and choice of interval when composed. For instance the interval of the augmented fourth (C to F#), a sharp-dissonant interval was forbidden. It was called "Diabolis in Musica," or the "devil in music."

The Reformation introduced hymn singing to the congregation, and many folk songs of the era were furnished with new lyrics, fit for singing in church. When criticized for adapting even local drinking songs to new hymns, Martin Luther is credited with saying, "Why should the devil have all the good tunes?" Additional emphasis was placed on new intervals, mostly mild dissonant intervals of the second, minor seventh and ninth.

Negro spirituals and gospel music added many new dimensions to the use intervals, particularly the occasional use of sharp dissonances and compound intervals. This added tension and excitement which was appropriate to the physical worship-style of the black church.

## Dangerous Intervals?

Unlike rhythm, there are no "dangerous" intervals. However, misuse of intervals and an overuse of sharp-dissonant intervals will create tension and sometimes anger, two emotions we usually are trying to calm and pacify during our worship services.

## Testing

- ❖ Have the choir or praise singers sing or hum a song or chorus without accompaniment and on a neutral syllable (no lyrics).
- ❖ Do the intervals enhance the meaning of the words or do they distract from them?
- ❖ Are there sharp-dissonances and large interval leaps (permissible if not overused)?
- ❖ Is the feeling you get listening to just the melody the same feeling you get from reading the words of the song?
- ❖ Does the melody by itself sound altogether lovely, inspirational, moving, spiritual?

## Summary

Intervals tend to soothe or disturb, depending on what the interval is that is being used. Sometimes we want to disturb musically, when we are singing about sin, persecution, judgment, and God's righteous anger. Just be sure the words and the intervals being used match in their emotional intent. Again, constant repetition of an interval, a lyric, and/or a rhythm is dangerous and has pagan, not biblical, roots.

> But when ye pray, use not vain repetitions, as the heathen do: for they think that they shall be heard for their much speaking.
>
> —Matthew 6:7

### Countermelody

Commit thy works unto the LORD, and thy thoughts shall be established.

—Proverbs 16:3

After rhythm, melody, and form, the next most common musical ingredient is what is called *countermelody*. The simple definition of this is: one or more melodies being played at the same time, but designed to compliment each other.

Some of the simplest and most familiar countermelodies are what we call "rounds," a song form where one group begins the melody, another enters a few measures later (with the same melody), and so on. Some simple folk song rounds include "Row Row Row Your Boat" and "Frere Jacques."

In contemporary Christian music, the most constant and obvious countermelody occurs between the actual melody of the song and the bass line. In rock–pop music (the source of most contemporary Christian music styles), the bass line is second in importance only to the melody.

Often in a rock (CCM) bass line, a single musical idea, usually two to four measures in length, is repeated over and over while the original melody above it evolves and changes. In earlier classical musical forms, this short repeated bass line is often called a *Chaconne,* or *Passacaglia,* sometimes a *bass-*

*ostinato.* The recent revival of a famous early classical piece, Pachelbel's "Canon" is a good example of the use of this early classical music form.

This constant repetition of the bass line, deliberately monotonous, can produce a mild hypnotic state, making the listener less conscious of their individuality and more conscious of being part of a "group" experience. The dangers involved in this are that the more discerning, discriminating, and evaluating parts of your brain are lulled into complacency. In the church, this can be dangerous. False doctrine can be easily slipped in this way without a strong conscious awareness.

### Esalen

On the Monterey Peninsula, near Big Sur, is a New Age institute called *Esalen.* Since the 1960s it has been a "think-tank" and experimental lab for many New Age ideas. One of their applications was to bring supposedly up-tight corporate executive to Esalen, have them change into comfortable clothing (sweat pants), and sit in a circle. Each person was given a drum, and there were two or three basic rhythm patterns distributed among the players. The lead drummer would begin the pattern and introduce the other patterns slowly until there was a multilayered pattern of syncopated but synchronized rhythms very similar, if not identical to, African drumming.

The purpose and the result of this exercise was the breakdown of individual consciousness and identity, substituted with a "collective consciousness" that was supposed to be "liberating." Unfortunately, this is not a new practice. Ancient religious cults throughout history have used similar techniques.

It is *always* dangerous to surrender individual consciousness to a group identity. You lose your sense of "self" and are very susceptible to ideas and behavioral practices you would never accept in your "own" mind. Christianity *never* asks you to do this. In fact, we are warned against it. To see these same practices enter the sanctuary of our churches is very disturbing. We must ask who and what is behind these supposedly "new" ideas, and what biblical support do they have?

## Be Yourself

Christ *never* wants us to be less of ourselves. Just the opposite in fact. Being "born again" frees you from worldly influences and helps you to become more "you," the very special, unique, and precious person that God created. Just as there are no two snowflakes that are identical, there has never been two identical human beings. Think about it. If God wanted a race of clones, He would have made us that way. On the other hand, Satan *always* attacks individuality, because it stands in the way of the teachings of false doctrine and the worship (by osmosis) of him.

## Summary

The hypnotic spell cast by repetitive rhythms, layered and repeated over and over, has crept into Christian music. The dangers, as outlined above, are increasingly apparent, as we see too many contemporary Christians who are ignorant of the word and the basic tenants of their faith, constantly looking for a religious "experience," a group "ecstacy" that is historically and musically the exact *opposite* of the basic tenants of our Christian beliefs.

### Harmony

Let them praise the name of the LORD: for his name alone is excellent; his glory is above the earth and heaven. He also exalteth the horn of his people, the praise of all his saints; even of the children of Israel, a people near unto him. Praise ye the LORD.

—Psalm 148:13–14

Harmony, sweet harmony! *Harmony* is the sound of two or more notes being sounded at the same time with the same rhythm. When three or more notes are sounded you have what is called a *chord*.

Chords are usually built on intervals of a third. For instance a "C" chord would select the first, third, and fifth note of the C scale: $C$ - D - $E$ - F - $G$ - A - B - C — C E G = "C" chord. Three-note chords are called *triads*. Chords with four notes are called *sixths* (C6) or *sevenths* (C7). Chords can be built on intervals other than thirds, the most common being chords built on fourths, but most traditional and even most contemporary Christian music have chords built on thirds.

A *chord progression* is when one chord changes to another chord. These harmonic changes, underneath the melody and above the bass line, create a musical "fullness" and support both the melody and the countermelody. The most common chord progression in traditional church music is the chord built on the first note of the scale (C), moving to a chord built on either the fourth note of the scale (F) or the fifth note of the scale (G). The chord built on the fifth note of the scale is often a four-note chord, indicated by marking it as a *G7* chord.

The primary chord progression of C-F-C-G7-C (order may change) is the harmonic superstructure under most traditional hymns and spirituals. Other chords may be used, and these same chords will change when the melody moves from a "major" tonality to a "minor" tonality, but this basic chord progression is the most common.

### Modal Progressions

Contemporary Christian music not only introduced many foreign rhythms, but it is also responsible for turning to modal scales and harmony, as did many of the early rock 'n roll groups like the Beatles. The more exotic-sounding modes and scales are more traditional to other cultures. The chord progressions in these new modes usually move in a *linear* manner (up and down the scale) rather than the more traditional motion of moving by fourths and fifths.

A commonly used modal scale is called the *dorian* mode (scale). Notes for a dorian scale could be: D-E-F-G-A-B-C-D; in other words, just starting on the second note of a C scale and going up eight notes will produce a *dorian* scale.

The most common chord progression in this new mode or scale would be a chord built on the first note of the scale, moving up to a chord built on the second note of the scale, moving up to a chord built on the third note of the scale, and back down. This is *linear* progression: First (D-F-A) — second (E-F-G) — third (F-A-C) — and back down.

The use of modal scales and linear chord progressions intensifies the potentially hypnotic effect of the music, especially when combined with repetitive rhythms, melodies, and lyrics. There is nothing potentially dangerous in linear chord progressions or modal scales, but they tend to be overly repetitive in application, more intent in creating a "mood" than leading musical and lyrical ideas to their logical conclusion.

A great deal of what we call "New Age" music today uses modal scales and linear chord progressions. New Age music abandons any intention of developing a logical idea through the elements of form, melody, and harmony, but instead falls back on Eastern and in many instances occult uses of music to create a hypnotic effect, a musical force field that transports the listener into supposedly "new" levels of consciousness. This type of music is often combined with the use of hallucinogenic drugs and/or Eastern forms of hypnotic meditation. All are deadly dangerous to the Christian and are the antithesis of true spiritual growth and consciousness.

### Warning
We all understand that music, like the other art forms, searches

for new ways to express our feelings, ways that are more in tune with our culture, our conditioning, and our environment. However, music, being the most powerful of all the art forms, and the one where there can be no conscious censorship, is most susceptible to psychic manipulation of individual consciousness through these potentially hypnotic techniques.

### Summary

There have been many deeply spiritual and moving contemporary Christian praise songs written over a modal scale and chord progression. However, in each instance there is a *strong* lyric, an evolving melody, and simple rhythm patterns, allowing us to enjoy this new musical style without sacrificing our individual consciousness.

New Age music attempts to capture a mood rather than give us a melody and a normal harmonic progression. Often, the chord progressions in New Age music are simple, repetitious, and monotonous — again, a danger to those of us who want to be *more* conscious rather than less. I don't think, when we go into the throne room of the Creator of the universe (through the power of the shed blood of Jesus Christ on the cross of Calvary) that we want to be "doped" up — we want to be alert and happy!

## Texture

It is better to hear the rebuke of the wise, than for a man to hear the song of fools.

—Ecclesiastes 7:5

The sixth element in music is called *texture*. Texture is made up of two main ingredients: 1) tone color and 2) register (high or low). Many changes have taken place in these two areas in Christian music in the past fifty years or more.

### Tone Quality

*Five Tone-Colors.* There are five basic tone colors in music:

❖ Bright (metallic, brittle, edgy, piercing)
❖ Clear (brilliant but not edgy, beautiful sound)
❖ Dark (muffled, rich in tone-quality)
❖ Raspy (buzz tone — like the voice of Louis Armstrong)
❖ Distorted (electronic distortion of basic tone quality)

Again, the choice of tone quality will reinforce or weaken the overall musical message you are trying to send. The more co-ordinated the musical elements are the *stronger the impact of the music.* That's why simple songs, that are well-coordinated in the seven or eight elements of music often have a more emotional and artistic impact than those that knowingly or unknowingly send contradictory messages. For instance, "Amazing Grace" is perfectly balanced between lyric, melody, etc., hence its strong message. The same could be said for "A Mighty Fortress Is Our God."

*New Colors.* Traditional church music relied, for the most part, on the two tone colors of *clear* and *dark,* with an occasional escape into *bright.* Influenced by the twanging guitars of rock and the blues–jazz sounds, many contemporary artists and recordings in Christian music have introduced bright, raspy, and distorted, as extreme forms of tonal expression. These are of African origin and are designed to heighten and intensify (exaggerate) the emotions being expressed by the song. Emotional exaggeration is a characteristic of rock and pop music today.

These new colors are often startling, distracting, and over-emotionalized in their use. They can often distract from the lyric, melody, or harmonic structure. Today in rock music, the tonal distortion is every bit as important as the lyric or melo-dy. In fact, in many instances, like "rap" music, there is no melody at all.

Some of these sounds grew out of black gospel music as well. Within the context of the genre (black gospel), they are exciting and appropriate. When applied without discretion to other musical styles they can be distracting and disturbing.

## *Register*

Traditional church music generally stayed within the register of the human voice; i.e. low "F" (below bass clef) to high "C" (two octaves above middle C). These are the parameters of the bass voice (low) up through the soprano voice (high).

The use of the organ and the piano in church extended the register possibilities another octave either way (low or high). The mighty power of the organ, underneath the exciting full-voiced choir, is still one of the most musically exciting and thrilling sounds possible. It's a shame to see it no longer represented in many of the more contemporary church worship services.

Low register musical vibrations carry farther and have more power than any other register. They also can affect internal organs and the endocrine gland system. The often insensitive use of the electric bass in church praise bands can be producing a physical response, particularly among the young, that is often in direct contradiction to the feelings of awe, respect, and love that we are trying for when we worship our Lord and Savior. One of the most constant abuses I hear with praise bands is in this area.

Loud, low, repetitive, and syncopated bass patterns trigger physiological and emotional responses that are more associated with pep rallies, discos, dancehalls, and sensual dancing than worship. Remember, if it walks like a duck, squawks like a duck, and looks like a duck, it's probably a duck. If it sounds like a rock band, over-emotionalizes like a rock band, and looks like a rock band, it is a rock band — now called a "praise" band.

Just hanging a "religious" lyric on it won't help. The musical style will overpower the lyric and even the melody. It's sad to realize how few pastors and music directors realize this. Again, it's no accident that this style of music has been looked upon with suspicion by the church for centuries.

High register sounds can be piercing, particularly if they are produced with a "bright" tone. Wailing electric guitars, screaming trumpets, shrill flutes, or soprano saxes — all trigger the instinctual "fight-or-flight syndrome" through our auditory and endocrine gland system, resulting in a congregation that is ready to run, fight, or dance rather than worship.

### Summary

Again, your own common sense and emotional response to the music should be your guide. Much of the contemporary Christian music brought into the sanctuary should have been left on the concert stage. There are many young Christian musical groups that are going out and witnessing to the lost through their own music (the unsaved). This is a legitimate and important evangelical outreach. However, that *does not* mean that this music is transferable to the worship service. More discretion needs to be applied in deciding what is "concert" music and what is appropriate "worship" music.

> Many will say to me in that day, Lord, Lord, have we not prophesied in thy name? and in thy name have cast out devils? and in thy name done many wonderful works? And then will I profess unto them, I never knew you: depart from me, ye that work iniquity.
>
> —Matthew 7:22–23

## Style

> *Even so ye, forasmuch as ye are zealous of spiritual gifts, seek that ye may excel to the edifying of the church.
>
> —1 Corinthians 14:12

Our seventh element of music is *style*. Style is made up of three components:

- ❖ Dynamics (loud and soft)
- ❖ Tempo (slow or fast)
- ❖ Articulation (smooth or short-detached)

## Dynamics

*No Contrast.* One of the greatest criticisms I have of much of what I hear in the church today in the way of contemporary Christian music is the *lack of dynamic contrast.* Pop-rock was designed for FM-AM radio and dancing. In both instances, subtle and musically important changes in musical style involving dynamics would be lost on the audience. In fact, they would resent it.

When you're driving through heavy traffic, listening to your favorite music station, it's annoying when the volume level drops suddenly. You either have to set the volume level so high that the loud passage hurt your ears or so low you miss the soft passages. That's one of the reasons classical music has not translated well to AM radio.

Most classical music has a wide range of dynamics, from super softs to thundering louds. These dynamic contrasts are thrilling in a concert hall or sitting at home listening on an expensive sound-reproduction system. In a disco or on the freeway in your automobile, or listening as background music at work or in the market, it's frustrating.

As a result, most pop-rock music today has little or no dynamic contrast. It's like having a person converse with you at the top of their voice. It's annoying, distracting, and it certainly destroys any other musical subtleties by the constant loud sound. Too much contemporary Christian music follows this format.

*Soft–Loud.* Soft sounds suggest intimacy; loud sounds suggest aggression or danger. A song with an intimate lyric played loudly will wipe out the meaning of the lyric and vice versa. To compound the problem, we have a young generation today, of which experts estimate up to twenty-five percent suffer some hearing loss from listening to or playing rock music or being around loud engines, tools, etc. Many of our young congregation today cannot *hear* the music if it is played softly.

*Effect.* The next time you are someplace where you won't distract folks, recite the Lord's Prayer out loud *at the top of your voice.* Note the effect. Then go back and recite the prayer, using soft and loud where appropriate. Hear the difference? *You lose the subtleties of meaning when the prayer is recited loudly.* The same thing can be said for a musical performance that is basically loud and louder.

### Tempo

Like dynamics, there are great contrasts in most great traditional church and classical music tempos. Classical music offers tempo that go as low as forty-four beats per minute (slower than counting seconds) and as fast as two hundred beats per minute (almost four beats per second).

Most pop music has a much more limited tempo range. Slow tunes are seldom slower than seventy-two beats per minute (the level of a normal pulse beat) and fast tunes almost never go beyond one hundred sixty beats per minute (slightly faster that two beats per second). In most pop-rock bands, and many praise bands today, there are three common tempos:

- ❖ Slow (around seventy-two beats per minute)
- ❖ Medium (around one hundred twenty beats per minute)
- ❖ Fast (around one hundred sixty beats per minute)

This gives a certain monotony and predictability that often distracts from the deeper meaning of the lyrics. We must keep in mind that pop-rock music is basically *dance* music, and as such will *not* speed up or slow down in a song. The same can be said to be true in most contemporary Christian music.

The most *natural* thing you want to do when listening, particularly to the medium or fast contemporary Christian music songs when played with a rock beat by a rock ensemble is to *move your body,* snap your fingers, clap your hands, wiggle your hips, stomp your feet — *it is dance music and it is designed to produce this effect.* That's why older people in church are confused; they came to worship, not dance. They *do not* want to be emotionally stimulated in this way. It is the *antithesis* of why they go to church. It's also very characteristic of the described musical styles accompanying pagan religions popular at the time of Christ and the development of the early church. The early church fathers kept telling Christians to *come out* of the world system. I don't think this means to sneak the world system's musical styles into the church.

Music should imitate speech. We *do not* speak in a constant, syncopated manner unless we are a "rap" or "calypso" singer. Our speech should flow, subject to appropriate pauses, slowing down, and accelerating to making a point. Our music should follow this pattern and not be locked into the three standard tempos of rock dance music. All great art shows a balance between unity and variety. Too much unity and you have predictability; too much variety and you lose the continuity of the musical or lyrical idea. *Balance* is the key.

### Articulation

Smooth notes versus short, detached notes — those are the two extremes in articulation. Again, following the example of speech. We tend to speak in a smooth, fluid manner when we are praying and worshipping. Short, separated notes are more dramatic, suggesting danger, anger, or violence.

When I composed music for Hollywood films, it was important that the rhythms, tempos, and articulations used in a particular scene matched the physical action on the screen. If I was scoring a fight, short, syncopated, loud sounds were appropriate. If I was scoring a love scene, smooth, connected unsyncopated music worked better. Matching the *kinesthetic* movements on the screen to the music was vitally important.

Most of us associate worship with kinesthetic repose — an inward, contemplative state that involves little physical movement. Whatever physical movements that occur are certainly smooth, not aggressive. It is vitally important that the articulation used in the music *supports* this. Whenever the music is out of sync with the scene in a Hollywood film, the music actually *weakens* the dramatic impact of the scene instead of strengthening it. Many Hollywood films have been ruined by musical soundtracks that are not in sync with the emotions or physical actions taking place on screen.

### *Summary*
Musical style, which we now know includes dynamics, tempo, and articulation, represents the icing on the cake of a musical composition. The correct choice in musical style is vital to enhancing and bringing out the deeper meanings hidden in the music. Stylistic patterns that are in conflict with the music or the mood you wish to create are damaging to the overall affect and impact, not only of the music, but of whatever is happening or is about to happen "on-screen" (in the pulpit) as well.

> How is it then, brethren? when ye come together, every one of you hath a psalm, hath a doctrine, hath a tongue, hath a revelation, hath an interpretation. Let all things be done unto edifying.
>
> —1 Corinthians 14:26

# The Power of Music

In the beginning God created the heaven and the earth. And
the earth was without form, and void; and darkness was
upon the face of the deep. And the Spirit of God moved upon
the face of the waters. And God said, Let there be light: and
there was light.

—Genesis 1:1–3

Recently, in an experimental laboratory at the University of
California, Los Angeles, scientists experimented with sound
waves broadcast over small contained tanks of water. After
much experimentation, they were eventually able to produce
*light* from sound (at a certain frequency) over the water. They
were also able to "disturb" the water with sound waves at
certain frequencies.

## Sound

Music is sound vibrating at certain frequencies. Each human
being has a particular frequency of vibration for his or her
body. Each inanimate object also has its vibration frequency.
Years ago, in a midwestern town, a large smokestack was built
for a smelter plant in town. To speed the smoke through the
smokestack, the engineers installed a large circulating fan near
the base that was designed to pull the smoke through the

smokestack at a faster rate. When they turned the fan on, the entire smokestack began vibrating. Fearing the collapse of the smokestack, they called in an acoustical expert who told them that the frequency of the fan's vibrations was identical to the frequency of the smokestack, thus resulting in the sympathetic vibration. By changing the speed of the fan they were able to remove the danger of possibe collapse.

## The Physics of Sound

The body not only "hears" music through the auditory system, it "feels" music through the vibrations penetrating the body. Helen Keller, the famous blind deaf-mute, used to "listen" to music by placing her hand on a violin or piano when it was being played. The ancient cultures of India, Egypt, and Greece, used music for medicinal purposes where certain types of music were prescribed for particular ailments.

We've already established in our chapter on rock music the dangers of sudden, sharp, loud sounds which trigger the body's "fight-or-flight" response. What science has yet to determine are the deleterious effects of certain sounds on the internal organs of the body and the brain. In 1988, Dr. Guzzetta proposed the notion that musical vibrations that are in tune with our human vibratory pattern could have a profound healing effect on the entire body. As a result, the growing music therapy research is increasingly sustaining Dr. Guzzetta's hypothesis.

Researchers have known for a long time now that listening to music can directly influence pulse, blood pressure, and the electrical activity of muscles. Neuroscientists now suspect that some types of music can actually help build and strengthen connections among nerve cells in the cerebral cortex. A recent study showed that listening to the music of Mozart before an IQ test could boost the scores by roughly nine points (University of California, Irvine, 1993).

In 1987, Dr. Richman studied the sounds made by Gelada monkeys. They were observed to produce a wide variety of sounds of different pitches accompanying all their social interactions. Different rhythms, accents, and types of vocalization were used by the monkeys. Most interesting was the observation that the particular type of sound which an individual produced indicated the *current emotional state of the monkey.*

Continuing his research, Dr. Richman concluded that when tensions arose between individual monkeys they were often resolved by *synchronizing and coordinating vocal expressions.* Dr. Richman further concluded that humans, like monkeys, have discovered that songs sung together provide a *shared form of emotion* that allows the singers to share similar emotional responses. In other words, group singing provides a shared form of emotion. (Richman B., 1987, *Rhythm and Melody in Gelada Vocal Exchanges, Primates* 28(2): 199-223)

## Music and the Brain

Recent research, using magnetic resonance imaging (MRI), revealed that certain parts of the brains of professional musicians were larger than normal. The parts enlarged differed slightly according to the instrument played and how long the person had played that instrument.

A few years ago a Russian scientist developed an educational training program called "Super-Learning." Using slow, classical music playing in the background, along with students seated in comfortable chairs, the lecturer would present the material in a well-modulated, pleasant, but soft voice. Forbidden to take notes, the students were astounded to discover that their retention levels had doubled or tripled.

## Teenagers and Music

Martin Gardiner of Brown University recently reported at a national conference the results of a major study of the affects of music study on the general population. Tracking people in Rhode Island from birth until the age of thirty, they checked the relationship between arrest records of teenagers and the degree of involvement in music.

Gardiner found that the greater the involvement in music, *the lower the arrest record.* Teens who had music education *were less likely to get into trouble than students who didn't.* However, those who also were involved in playing a musical instrument had even *fewer* brushes with the law. Those who had the most experience, including good sight reading ability (most rock musicians can't read music) had a *negligible arrest record* (Musica Research Notes, Vol VII, Issue I, Winter, 2000, p. 2).

## Music as a Weapon

When the United States invaded Panama to unseat its unscrupulous drug dealing leader, Colonel Manuel Noriega, military intelligence used rock music, broadcast at earsplitting levels into his compound to speed his surrender.

A national chain of convenience-stores recently adopted the policy of playing light classical music broadcast softly just outside their stores to drive away gang activity. It seems that Mozart softened the gang's edge and took away their aggression.

The United States government has long been experimenting with sound as a weapon. With computers, we can quickly determine the vibrating frequency of any man-made object, broadcast a sympathetic vibration, and incapacitate that piece of equipment. Also, military troops in the field can be driven into fetal positions accompanied by nausea when certain sound waves are broadcast over their area. Soon, if not already, combat troops will be provided with ear plugs as well as gas masks.

## Music in Nursery School

Nursery schools have discovered that when selected classical music pieces are played during nap time, the children fall asleep sooner and achieve a deeper rest.

> Classical music has been a thirty-year staple at Les Petits Nursery in Brookline, Massachusetts, director Debra Nickerson said. And after years' worth of anecdotal evidence, Nickerson said, she has proof positive of one effect: Classical music helps kids nap.
>
> —*Mozart Effect,* Joanna Weiss, Boston Globe

## Music and Emotion

Music is the most powerful of all the arts because it is the most difficult to censor. Sound enters the ear, is processed through the auditory nerves, and enters the brain at mid-brain level, the hypothalamus. The brain has three levels. Level one is the thalamus, a small baseball-size area of the brain that sits atop the spine. It is the seat of all our automatic nervous system activities — breathing, circulating, digesting, etc. Above that level sits a larger core called the "hypothalamus." This part of the brain is called the "emotional" part of our brain — it is the seat of the emotions. The final area of the brain, the wrinkly part we see covering the other two, is called the "cerebrum." This part of the brain is the seat of knowledge, learning, and all the higher skills that separate man from the lower species.

Because music enters the mid-brain, you cannot censor your body's reaction to music. The only way you cannot react is to stop the music or plug the auditory canal with ear plugs. This is why music is so powerful. It is capable of seizing control of the individual, overpowering the higher senses of reason and logic in the hypothalamus, and cause people to do things their higher brain would object to. That's why I believe music can be used as a drug, and is probably the most dangerous drug we have on the market today.

Music's effect on the outer layers of the brain — the temporal and even the visual cortex - is only half the story, however. These are the places in which the signal is being dissected and processed. The place where it is having its most profound effect is in the brain's emotional core — the limbic system.

—*The Biology of Music*, Science and Technology, Internet

I find it interesting in the studies I have made on the recreational drugs commonly used today, that they all primarily affect the limbic system, the same system that music profoundly affects.

## Summary

We've already established the power of music, physiologically, psychologically, culturally, and spiritually. When combined with worship, which should be mainly the lifting up of His name in praise and song, you have the most powerful force, next to prayer, in the spiritual universe. It's no wonder that Satan works overtime to weaken, confuse, and mislead worship leaders.

Throughout the Bible we are given startling and exciting examples of the power of music — everything from a praise choir defeating an overwhelming invading army (2 Chron. 20) to the bringing down of the Shekinah Glory on the newly built Temple of Solomon (2 Chron. 5:13–14). An entire chapter, First Chronicles 25 is devoted to showing the detailed assignments of the singers within the Temple. All musicians were selected from the Levites; indicating the singers and musicians were considered as important as priests and required the same sanctification and purification rituals.

I believe that we are just beginning to discover the amazing power of music and sound. I believe one of the great discoveries that will be made in this century will be the profound effects music has on the human body and the environment. When we really realize what certain types of music are doing to our young people there will be a hue and outcry against the recording industry and MTV that will make the uproar over cigarette smoking seem tame by comparison. In the meantime, we have an obligation to our congregations not to let the wolf into the sheepfold, whether it be through music, false teachings, or other ways that Satan is constantly trying in his efforts to weaken the church of Jesus Christ.

# The World and the Church

And I say also unto thee, That thou art Peter [Petros, "little" rock], and upon this rock [Petra, "big" rock — Jesus the rock of salvation] I [Jesus, not Peter] will build my church; and the gates of hell shall not prevail against it.

—Matthew 16:18

Historically, the church was always a place where one could run to escape the world. Real or imaginary, there was a sense of "holiness," "unworldliness," about the church, a place where time stood still in awe and wonder of the awesomeness of God and His power. Today that is no longer the case. It's increasingly harder to tell the church from the world or vice versa

## Marriage

A recent article in the *Kansas City Star* newspaper (November 12, 1999, p. A-1) states the following:

Aside from the quickie-divorce Mecca of Nevada, no region of the United States has a higher divorce rate than four Bible Belt states; Tennessee, Arkansas, Alabama and Oklahoma. In a country where nearly half of all marriages break up, the divorce rates in these states are about *50 percent above the national average.*

A startling trend. Apparently the "holiness" of God and the sanctity of marriage have both failed in four of the most Christian fundamentalist states in our nation.

What has this to do with music in the church? A lot. I believe that there is no longer a place, with few exceptions, where people can go and experience this holiness. I also believe that the turning to worldly musical styles, with the rational that it will more likely attract the unsaved and keep the young people happy, has failed. Rather, it has lowered the standards of holiness as expressed through music and worship to the point where only the lyrics of these songs indicate *any* recognition of the divine and often these lyrics are so simplistic and insulting to a Holy God that they alienate rather than attract those truly wishing to experience the divine.

## Defining Holiness in Worship

The Rev. Daniel D. Meyer, senior pastor of Christ Church of Oak Brook, Illinois, said recently in a church bulletin regarding the criteria for guiding the selection of music in the worship service:

> We will continue to view either an empty emotionalism or a passionless formalism to be incompatible with excellent worship.

In that one sentence Rev. Meyer has defined the two extremes in church music today: on the one hand, an emotional but "empty" (and often disrespectful) attempt at worship through music, and on the other a "boring" formalism that is just as much of an insult to the divine as the other.

## Come Out from Them

Over and over, the Holy Bible tells true believers to "come out from them!" What does that mean? Does it mean we are to wear funny underwear like the Mormons, worship on Saturday or face damnation as the Seven Day Adventists believe, or to maintain regular taking of communion or face the loss of our salvation as taught by the Catholic Church? None of the above. It is to realize that our citizenship is no longer on earth but in heaven. Our treasures are there not here. Earth is just a place we are passing through.

The symbolism of baptism is death to self and re-emergence as a new person, dedicated to living a life of holiness (only with the help of the Holy Spirit) that will attract others. Paul the apostle and the early church used to tell non-believers, "come and live with us — watch us — see how different we are from the world!" Can we do that today? What if our music, along with our attitudes and dress, are symbolic of worldliness, not holiness? Why should anyone bother to become part of what they already are?

### Fear

Proverbs teaches us that "the beginning of wisdom is the fear (awe and wonder) of God." Recently I did a teaching in my Bible class on "fear." I believe that the worldliness that has wandered into the church is partly the result of the loss of fear for our Maker. Paul the apostle said we are to work out our salvation with "fear and trembling." Why? Can we lose our salvation? No, but we can lose our sense of the holiness of God and what He represents. Fear also reminds us of what we are saved *from* (hell) as well as what we are saved *for* (heaven).

### Approval

I loved my physical father, and I *feared* his withdrawal of approval of me and my behavior, not so much because of the punishment, but more because I suddenly felt lonely, cut-off from the approval I so desperately needed to succeed. I believe we should have a similar feeling of being "cut off" from the Divine presence of our spiritual Father through sin. Whenever we put the approval of man above the approval of God we will be "cut off" from the power of the Holy Spirit — until we realize this fact, confess our sin, repent (turn from our sin), and ask our spiritual father to forgive us.

How does this apply to music? Whenever we select music that was not conceived, inspired, and birthed through a deep respect for the holiness of God we have sought worldly approval rather than spiritual. Whenever the style, the lyric, the melody, and the presentation does not make the performer or the congregation more aware rather than less of the overpowering holiness of God, we have failed in our mission.

> Churches all over America are being torn apart over the issue of music. The easy movement from the treasure of our hymnody of the past into to banal, meterless, mostly meaningless repetitious monotony of today's chorus approach, bespeaks an ignorance of our historical treasure, as well as our musical evolution (or better yet, devolution), over time.
> —Dr. Lane Adams, former assistant to Billy Graham

Whenever you wander through the great cathedrals of Europe, you are struck with the sense that the builders were trying, in their pitiful human way, to capture a bit of the essence of God. You also sense a deep humility. One does not find a person's name carved underneath most statues, glass windows, or organ installations. They chose to remain anonymous — in their true humility and respect for God.

No one knows, for instance, the authors of hundreds of Gregorian chants and early hymns that were sung by the church. No one knows who wrote (with few exceptions) the melodies upon which the psalms of David were sung in the Temple in Jerusalem by the ancient Hebrews.

I see so much pride in Christian music today. Having served as a clinician, lecturer, and performer at many of the top Christian gatherings, I have seen very little humility and a lot of pride from the film industry in Hollywood. Compared to the Christian music industry, I am increasingly seeing very little difference between the two.

So often when I visit a church today with contemporary music, I find huge displays in the lobby of the sanctuary with the CDs, t-shirts, and posters of the "artist" who is "performing" that day in the sanctuary. There is something about this that bothers me. Yes, church musician's should be able to make a living, but turning the sanctuary into a commercial for their careers is bothersome.

The emphasis on very casual or bizarre dress is also bothersome. Paul the apostle took the Corinthian church to task for allowing their women to dress in such a manner that it was a distraction to the service. Today, torn Levis, t-shirts, nose and earrings (on men as well as on women), suggests a casualness that is repugnant to me, and I believe is disrespectful to God. Again, "no fear," equals "no respect."

I recently asked a well-known New York jazz musician (originally from New Orleans) why he and his group always appeared nattily attired in suits and ties for their performances. His answer was, "If you don't care enough for your art form to dress up as you would for church, you are sending the wrong signal to your audience." Yes, he was a black jazz musician, and yes, today the black church, for the most part, dresses for church — and their singers dress or are in choir robes. Do they realize something we don't?

## Summary

If there is one thing that music in a worship service should place above all, it is the job of inspiring, through music, the awe and wonder of God and *His holiness*. I sometimes wish I could ask the gyrating, banging, distorting, poorly-dressed praise band members and their gypsy-looking singers, "Would you dress, act, sing, and perform in this manner in front of your Creator?" If the answer was "no," then the next question would be, "Then who *are* you performing for now?"

> And they continued stedfastly in the apostles' doctrine and fellowship, and in breaking of bread, and in prayers. And fear came upon every soul: and many wonders and signs were done by the apostles. And all that believed were together, and had all things common; And sold their possessions and goods, and parted them to all men, as every man had need. And they, continuing daily with one accord in the temple, and breaking bread from house to house, did eat their meat with gladness and singleness of heart, Praising God, and having favour with all the people. And the Lord added to the church daily such as should be saved.
>
> —Acts 2:42–47

The loss of a sense of "holiness" during many contemporary Christian worship services cannot be exchanged for an emotional high. Neither can this loss of holiness be the price the church has to pay to attract and keep young people and non-believers. To believe that is to contradict the very foundation and purpose of religion. We have truly sold our spiritual heritage for a bowl of porridge.

# The Cults and Music

And Elijah said unto the prophets of Baal, Choose you one bullock for yourselves, and dress it first; for ye are many; and call on the name of your gods, but put no fire under. And they took the bullock which was given them, and they dressed it, and called on the name of Baal from morning even until noon, saying, O Baal, hear us. But there was no voice, nor any that answered. And they leaped upon the altar which was made.

—1 Kings 18:25–26

Other historical documents and research have assured us that these pagan rituals were almost always accompanied by loud, repetitious music, chanting, and dancing. The whole idea was to place the priests or the dancers into a hypnotic state through which demons could enter and help them perform supposedly supernatural tricks. In the presence of the one true God of the universe they are rendered impotent. Also in Christ's marvelous message called the *Sermon on the Mount* (Matt. 5–7) when instructing His disciples on how to pray, He cautions them not to use "vain repetitions, as the heathen do." What did He mean, "vain repitions, as the heathen do"?

Repetitious rhythms, lyrics, and simplistic melodies are

conducive to induce hypnosis. Advanced states of hypnosis are typical of most of the cults. It's only when one surrenders control of their higher, logical, emotionally-controlled mind that false doctrine can be introduced into the subconscious. When one reads the doctrinal statements of these cults and false religions, many of the statements are ludicrous and laughable. How could *anyone* in their right mind believe that stuff? The key words are *right mind.*

Just as advertising agencies on Madison Avenue in New York City learned long ago, music can influence you to (a) remember the name of their product, (b) be unconsciously drawn toward buying their product, and (c) remain loyal to their product — all through the bonding process of music.

Today children do not learn nursery rhymes so much as they learn songs from television ads. Even today, most of you, if you try, can come up with five to ten melodies that you still remember for products advertised on television even though the product itself may no longer be available or the company now uses a different melody for product identification. For instance:

- ❖ "You wonder where the yellow went, when you brush your teeth with Pepsodent"
- ❖ "See the USA in your Chevrolet!"
- ❖ "When You Wish Upon a Star" (Disneyland)
- ❖ "Thanks for the Memory" (Bob Hope Show)

Once planted, these songs live a long time in your long-term memory (right brain). Today this technique is being used very successfully and rightly so in teaching scripture to young children in Sunday school. They are *taught* to sing the scripture to a catchy but simple melody. Religious cults often teach their basic doctrine through song, chanting, or repetition, to guarantee long- term memory. Unfortunately, this long-term memory does not know right from wrong, is divorced from the logical mind, and will accept anything fed into it.

## Warning Signs

Any time you are asked to chant, recite, or sing simplistic slogans and statements over and over, you are bypassing the critical mind and are going directly to the subconscious. This is a standard characteristic of most cults. They require, often daily or even several times a day, the chanting, speaking, or singing of simplistic doctrinal statements. Each time that happens, it drives that statement deeper into the unconscious mind.

That's why it is sometimes necessary to hire a professional deprogrammer when parents or friends are successful in rescuing a family member from a cult. Their mind has literally been programmed to accept nonsense and requires deprogramming — mental detoxification — to bring them back to a normal state of consciousness. Again, that's why Christ warned us not to *use vain repetitions, as the heathen do.*

Strong, sensuous rhythms can intensify and emotionalize the message. If it "feels good," it must be okay. One of the slogans of the 1960s was: "If it feels good, do it!" Many did, and the results have been catastrophic. Drug addiction, sexual diseases, suicide, alcoholism, sexual perversion, occult activities, and even demonic or satanic worship — all are byproducts of this type of activity.

## World Religions

Which of the major religions of the world uses mindless repetition, with or without music to drive home basic doctrine?

* Islam (call-to-prayer; five times a day)
* Buddhism (chanting, prayer beads, sometimes with droning music)
* Hinduism (oldest major religion uses this technique regularly, hours a day — Raja Yoga)

❖ Taoism (chanting, use of repetitious rhythms)
❖ Shintoism (Japanese warrior religion)
❖ Catholicism (rosary beads, repetitious chants)
❖ African tribal religions (dancing, chanting, music — very syncopated, repetitious)
❖ Voodoo (Haiti — repetitious chanting, dancing, syncopated drums)
❖ Santaria (Cuba — same as above plus sacrifice of animals)
❖ Macumba (Brazil — same as above)
❖ Polynesian religions (native Hawaiian, Samoan, New Zealand)
❖ Aborigines (Australia)
❖ Native American religions (North and South America)
❖ Chinese communism (under Mao)
❖ Nazi ceremonies, rituals, chants
❖ Russian communism (under Stalin)
❖ New Age religions

Logical human beings can be programmed to do illogical things and accept illogical doctrine through these techniques. Basically, the rhythmic, repetitious chanting — with or without music — overrides the conscious mind and feeds thoughts, beliefs, and often a call to action to those being conditioned.

I have seen videotapes of the so-called "Toronto Blessing" and the so-called revivals of the Pensacola, Florida, "Brownsville Pentecostal Church." *The same techniques used by cults and forbidden by Jesus Christ are used to debase Christianity and the whole concept of spiritual revival.* These tapes are disturbing. They use the identical occult techniques outlined above for "spiritual" awakening. The Devil must be laughing himself sick when he sees Christians barking like dogs, howling like wolves, knocked over like bowling pins, and *wanting more.*

It is one thing to see these practices on film and television, and in-the-field experiences in some foriegn country. It is another to see them in a Christian church in America, and to see them be so readily accepted by a wide range of pastors and denominations as being biblically credible when they are (obvious to most) just the opposite. Whether it is done in some empty field in Haiti at midnight, or a diluted version in a so-called Christian church, these practices are historically and demonstrably demonic in nature and are the antithesis of true Christianity. Christ came to free us from this kind of bondage, not to deliver us up to the adversary.

In the Olivet Discourse (Matt. 24–25; Mark 13; Luke 21) Christ outlines the signs and conditions that will precede His second coming. The one sign He mentions and emphasizes more than any other is *spiritual deception*. Christ says that even the "very elect" may be deceived. I believe that music is being used to deceive the church and the saints. The lack of discrimination in musical use in the church, and the lack of awareness of its dangers when used improperly, lead me to this belief.

Most cults that use repetitious music reinforce and intensify the experience with accompanying drum patterns. Whether these be the conga drums of Cuba, the tabla drums of India, or the drum set of the rock drummer, all syncopated, repetitious rhythms in church music are suspect, particularly when accompanied by drums. No one knows exactly why demons can be summoned by certain rhythmic patterns, but there is a mountain of field research, including film and video that proves that this is the case. Once again, that is why we in Christ's church must be alert to the types of rhythm used in worship services.

Today, many youth Christian rallies, revivals, and worship services are getting their attendees "high" by overstimulating the endocrine gland system, and in particular the adrenal glands. This high is often mistaken for a state of higher spiritual awareness. This aroused emotional state is being passed off as a sure sign of the presence of the Holy Spirit. Nothing could be further from the truth. When we read about the Holy Spirit, from the Book of Acts on, we *never* find that this important part of the Trinity can be summoned by drums, loud music, or repetitious singing.

That's why many believe these strange happenings in church to be real. The body has been changed, their conscious minds overridden, and they are ready to "experience" Christ instead of being led to understand Him. A phony physical (partly mental) spiritual high is mistaken for a manifestation of the Holy Spirit and spiritual growth. Again, nothing could be further from the truth.

Unfortunately, once pastors, worship leaders, congregations, and even denominations, start down this slippery path, it's hard to turn around. People get hooked on the experience and the high. Old fashioned worship practices seem dull and uninteresting. They are too low-key, subdued. Not enough excitement. Got to go where the "excitement" is, because that's where Jesus is! False reasoning, satanic deception.

## How to Destroy a Church

Satan has a three-pronged plan: deception, division, and destruction. First he deceives. In music he (a) weakens doctrine with simplistic, over-personalized lyrics, (b) uses repetition to put the conscious mind asleep, and (c) activates the adrenal glands through syncopated, loud rhythms (particularly drums), creating a synthetic religious experience. A false *emotional high* is thought to be an authentic *spiritual experience*. Once he has deceived a large number of the congregation he then proceeds to divide, by pitting the traditionalist against the innovator, the spiritually aware against the spiritually naive.

One of the primary reasons for churches splitting in these last days has been over the *music and worship service*. As stated earlier, today a church is more properly defined by the style and nature of its worship than by its denomination or pastor.

After Satan has succeeded in deceiving and dividing, he then sets out to destroy. He moves to destroy the traditionalist by making them bitter, withdrawing from communal spiritual life, staying at home watching some pumped-up, ecumenical, overly-emotional television evangelist or preacher. He leads the other contingent, those spiritually naive, over the cliff with an ever-increasing desire for greater and greater spiritual "highs" until they end up in apostasy, emotional turmoil, or a nervous breakdown. Either way the true church of Christ loses and Satan wins.

Satan's objective is to turn every body of believers either into a dead, apostate church (which he will leave alone or even help prosper) or to destroy a congregation and make individual believers pessimistic and spiritually dead in the water. Satan fears the power of the church more than any other force. Until Christ returns in the flesh, His power over the adversary is through the Holy Spirit active in every believer and the collective power of the believing church. Satan hates and fears this power. He will do *anything* he can to weaken the church or destroy it.

Besides the church, Satan fears the power of the next generation. He attacks heavily, just before and after puberty. He will do *everything* in his power to deceive young adults into not accepting Jesus Christ as their Lord and Savior. He knows the longer they wait, the less likely they are to make that decision. He attacks with everything he has, but one of his favorite weapons is contemporary pop music. Even if the church cleans up its act musically, many teenagers are being led literally into "hell" through the music they listen to. Parents today have an *awesome* responsibility to help their teenagers understand the dangers involved in listening to certain kinds of contemporary pop music.

## Summary

We need not fear that Satan will destroy the church. Christ promised in Matthew 16 that *the gates of hell* would not prevail against His church. On the other hand, Satan can certainly weaken the church and it's impact on contemporary society by deceiving, dividing, and destroying unity. Music is one of his favorite tools. We owe it to our youth to make them aware of spiritual warfare, particularly in the area of music. We must do everything we can to protect our young.

> And it came to pass at noon, that Elijah mocked them, and said, Cry aloud: for he is a god; either he is talking, or he is pursuing, or he is in a journey, or peradventure he sleepeth, and must be awaked.
>
> —1 Kings 18:27

# Spiritual Warfare and Music

Many contemporary Christians have naively forgotten, or have never been told that we, the body of Christ, the church, the bride of Christ, are in a twenty-four–hour–a–day spiritual battle with the forces of darkness. Through the blood of Jesus Christ, we have victory over these forces, but *only* if (a) we are truly born-again, (b) confess and repent of our sins daily, and (c) resist the temptations of the flesh and the seductiveness of the world.

> Love not the world, neither the things that are in the world. If any man love the world, the love of the Father is not in him. For all that is in the world, the lust of the flesh, and the lust of the eyes, and the pride of life, is not of the Father, but is of the world.
>
> —1 John 2:15–16

Satan is constantly working to (a) destroy the Jew, so Christ will have no nation of which to be "king" when He comes back, (b) destroy or control Israel and in particular Jerusalem, so Christ will have no city and Temple to call His own, (c) harass the true church, the bride of Christ through direct persecution or the introduction of false doctrine, and (d) keep as many human beings as possible from coming to a saving knowledge of Jesus Christ.

According to Ezekiel 28 and Isaiah 14, along with Daniel 11, we have some of the most complete descriptions available of who and what Satan (the adversary) was and is like. We know from these and other biblical passages that at one time Lucifer, the name of Satan before he fell, was *in charge of worship*. We also know from these passages that he had something *directly to do* with music, singing, and praising God.

Satan is *very aware* of how to mislead congregations, denominations, and apostate churches into false and even demonically-controlled worship. Being "slain in the spirit," barking like dogs, rolling around on the floor with uncontrollable laughter, moaning, losing consciousness, and the like, are being passed off these days as being indications of true manifestations of the Holy Spirit. *Nothing could be further from the truth.* These are demonic manifestations, more common to occult religions than Christianity. Yet these signs, often accompanied by "demonized" music, are being passed off as an authentic revival — an outbreak of the Holy Spirit in these latter days. Only the biblically illiterate and the spiritually immature buy into this. Unfortunately, that includes a lot of supposed Christians today.

There is a fight between the forces of darkness and the power of the Word of God in every authentic and scriptural-centered Christian religious service. The forces of darkness would like to bring about distractions, disagreements, misunderstandings, an out-and-out rebellion on the part of as many believers as they can reach. They will use music, lighting, distracting behavior, unusual dress — anything they can to weaken the impact of the Word of God and its spiritual clarification.

On the other hand, angels stand ready to help us resist these forces. How do we resist them? Through prayer, praise, lifting up the name of Jesus, and the Word of God. Music *should* be a unifying factor, not a *dividing* factor, in this struggle. If the name of Jesus is lifted up, respectfully and scripturally, in song and praise, the forces of darkness are forced to flee. They *cannot stand* to be in the presence of powerful praise, lifting up the name of our Savior.

When the worship part of the service is practiced properly, these forces of darkness are forced from the sanctuary. A sense of peace, joy, and well-being descends on the congregation, and distractions are held to a minimum. As a result, when the pastor reads the Word of God and expounds on it, the sermon goes to the heart rather than the head. The message speaks to the spirit, not just the intellect or the senses.

Congregations need to *know* that this is one of the most important aspects of worship. Everyone engaged in worship — the worship leader, the music director, the musicians and singers, the pastors, the congregation — all need to know that when worship begins, spiritual warfare begins. The winner will be decided by the manner and content of the worship and the attitude of those involved.

## Cleansing

At the time of Christ, before the Jewish priests were allowed into the inner courtyard where sacrifices took place, they had to go through a purification process. Those attending the service had to go through a cleansing process as well. Although symbolic, it was a reminder that (a) we are sinners and are not worthy of appearing before the living God without purification, and (b) only *after* this purification would God accept the sacrifices presented to Him. Over and over in scripture God stresses *obedience is better than sacrifice*. God rejects all religious worship when the worshipper is not purified and sanctified.

All those involved in presenting worship must take time *before* the worship service to get their hearts right with God.

Each person must confess their sins (in private prayer), repent of those sins, and ask God to ritually "cleanse" them so they are worthy to participate in worship. Pride must be surrendered and humility must be put on like a garment. Any attention on the part of the singers, musicians, worship leaders, or pastoral staff, to draw attention to themselves, to use their "worldly" charismatic gifts to give a "lift" to worship, must be surrendered. God must break us (our pride) before He can use us. You don't have to be a Christian to see the pride in Christian music today. The same limousines, the same adoring fans, the same emphasis on record sales and the flesh as we see in the world.

That is why it is so dangerous to turn our praise bands, organists, accompanists, music conductors, singers, and the like into Christian *entertainers*. So often I see body language on the part of so-called Christian "artists" that indicate that they have surrendered to pride rather than humility. Too often I have been aware, in my own personal experience, of persons living in direct disobedience to God and yet are allowed to be an integral part of worship.

*God will never honor this kind of worship.* Read the Old Testament prophet Jeremiah. The Jewish religion was almost entirely apostate just prior to their invasion by Babylon and the subsequent destruction of the Temple in Jerusalem and the leading of the Jews into captivity (586 B.C.). God rejects over and over their blemished sacrifices and prideful, sin-laden sacrifices.

## Serious Business

Leading or participating in worship is serious business. It's not the "David Letterman Show" with a few prayers and spiritual songs thrown in. It's not celebrity worship. It's not a showcase of up-and-coming Christian musical artists and singers. *It is spiritual warfare.* A denomination, pastor, church, worship team, or congregation that does not realize this is in serious difficulty, no matter how polished, smooth, or musically excellent their presentation.

More than anything else, your spiritual sensitivity and type of worship defines your church — more than your pastor, your buildings, your denomination, or your many committees and clubs. A church dies first in worship. Why? Because if the forces of darkness are not driven away at the beginning of the service they will enter the sanctuary, confuse the pastor, the congregation, and the worship team. They will begin leading that church slowly but surely toward apostasy, further and further from humble worship and biblically ordained procedures.

Ironically, this is more likely to happen during times of growth than times of decline. One of the single biggest mistakes made by the contemporary Protestant churches in America today is that growth is *always* a sign that the Holy Spirit is attracting new members. Often it is just the opposite.

Research studies today indicate that most church attendees today in the new "seeker-sensitive" churches do not want to dress for church; they want the music to entertain rather than edify; they want the pastor to stay away from in-your-face biblical truths; they do not wish to be reminded of their sins and the need to repent; and they want "have a nice day" sermons that drop simplistic psychological slogans into their unconscious minds that can guide their coming week at home, on the job, and in the community.

Many services take on the air of a religious television variety show: a little singing, a little dancing, a little drama, a spiritual pep talk, and even some humor thrown in. The commercials are the announcements and the offertory. In these churches one must be careful not to offend by singing traditional hymns, preaching the power of the blood, or the threat of hell to the unsaved. Heaven forbid! Entertain, soothe, and allow for social interaction.

## Music in Heaven

We are given glimpses in scripture into the heavenlies (Ezek. 1–2; Isa. 6; Rev. 4–5, etc.). In almost every instance, singing and praise are key components — songs praising our Lord and Savior along with praise of Him and for Him, no songs that indicate "Jesus is my buddy." Whether we like it or not, heaven seems to spend a lot of time in singing and praising the Lord. Have you ever asked yourself what kind of music that would be?

I often suggest to worship leaders and church music directors, as well as pastors, that the ultimate criteria for selecting appropriate music for worship service could and should be, "Will this song, hymn, or chorus be appropriate to sing in heaven?" "How will it be accompanied in heaven?" "Will heaven have one hundred thousand rock drummers playing a sensuous, syncopated beat, along with another hundred thousand electric bass players booming a hypnotic, repetitious bass line, two hundred thousand guitars, twanging, squeaking, and distorting, along with four hundred thousand singers, screaming lyrics while wearing nose rings, spiked hair, and torn Levis? I don't think so.

## Hell

By October 30, when Brian came to trial, the Stones had finished their new album, *Their Satanic Majesties Request,* during the recording of which Andrew Oldham, disaffected with the Stones — "More than a group . . . a way of life," he'd called them.

—*Keith*: Biography of Rolling Stones guitarist, p. 79

On the other hand, what do you think the music of "hell" will be like. Many of the top rock groups *already* boast and recognize that their music is more suited for hell than heaven. In fact, they make it clear that they want nothing to do with heaven. They see hell as one big party, with sex, drugs, and rock 'n roll as being the main ingredients. Boy, are they in for a big surprise!

## The Bridge

Music and worship bridge heaven and earth. Are we elevating our congregations toward heaven or are we leading them somewhere else? Have we forgotten the spiritual war that we *must* win to grow spiritually? Are we sobered by the responsibility that we have in leading praise and worship? Do we prepare for each service like we are going into battle (which we are), or do we prepare to "entertain" the congregation?

We are told in many scriptural passages to *come out* of the world. Instead, in too many instances we have brought the *world* into the church, often through music and worship, and have opened the door for the enemy, the accuser of the brethren, to enter our sanctuary and to begin twisting and dividing our church.

## Summary

Praise and worship should be approached with fear, trepidation, and much prayer. Without the spiritual protection that we receive through having accepted Christ, living lives covered and purified by the blood and sanctified music and lyrics, we are doomed to spiritual defeat, no matter how many people you have seated in your church.

Seek ye the LORD, all ye meek of the earth, which have wrought his judgment; seek righteousness, seek meekness: it may be ye shall be hid in the day of the LORD's anger.
—Zephaniah 2:3

Praise ye the LORD. Sing unto the LORD a new song, and his praise in the congregation of saints. Let Israel rejoice in him that made him: let the children of Zion be joyful in their King. Let them praise his name in the dance: let them sing praises unto him with the timbrel and harp. For the LORD taketh pleasure in his people: he will beautify the meek with salvation.

—Psalm 149:1–4

Then shall ye call upon me, and ye shall go and pray unto me, and I will hearken unto you. And ye shall seek me, and find me, when ye shall search for me with all your heart.

—Jeremiah 29:12–13

And go not after other gods to serve them, and to worship them, and provoke me not to anger with the works of your hands; and I will do you no hurt.

—Jeremiah 25:6

# Spiritual Power and Music

Then said Saul unto his servants, Seek me a woman that hath a familiar spirit, that I may go to her, and inquire of her. And his servants said to him, Behold, there is a woman that hath a familiar spirit at Endor.

—1 Samuel 28:7

Before I surrendered my life to Jesus Christ, (John 3), I was after spiritual "power." I sought this power through music, astrology, meditation, and other occult techniques. I found power, but it was the wrong kind. For every bit of power, I had to surrender another piece of my soul. I was being led into hell. Somehow, I sensed it, and in August 1973 I reached out in a small church in northern California and found the *real* power in the universe — Jesus Christ.

However, following my new spiritual path, reading the Bible, praying, seeking fellowship with other believers, being discipled, etc. I found that to have *real* spiritual power, the only kind that is not self-destructive, I had to surrender more and more of my pride, my ego, my attraction to the world and the flesh. In other words, as Christ said, to find your true self you have to lose your unreal self, the self of self-centeredness. Just as pride is the single greatest cause of sin, humility is the single greatest sign of true spiritual power.

There is no spiritual power in your life without Jesus Christ as your Lord and Savior, and without true humility, a humility that tries (and fails daily) to put Christ first, others second, and yourself last. Thank God we have a Savior that forgives our sin (when we repent), washes us clean, sets us upright, and encourages us to try again. Remember, our role model was a humble, suffering servant, who washed the feet of His disciples the night before His arrest and trial.

## Power in Music

We have already explored the seven different aspects of music and how they, individually and when combined correctly, can produce tremendous and powerful affects on our bodies, our minds, and our very souls. I would venture to say that Satan probably uses music as a tool to lead people to hell more than any other because he *knows* the power of music and how to twist that power to his advantage. He has practically destroyed more than one generation of young people through his twisted but powerful musical puppets.

On the other hand, we know that the power of Jesus Christ is superior to *any* other power in the universe and can *overcome* the very fires of hell when necessary. However, for Christian music to work, all seven parts must line up properly and the inspiration for the music must be Divine. When this happens, we have a musical product that can touch the hearts of even the most cold-hearted man or woman.

In this category is the worldly-popular and spiritually-inspired "Amazing Grace." This song was written by a former slave boat captain who experienced firsthand the awesome power of God in his life and captured the essence of his experience in his song:

> Amazing grace! How sweet the sound that saved a wretch like me.
> I once was lost, but now am found; was blind, but now I see.

John Newton goes on for five more verses, ending with one of the most musically moving descriptions of heaven ever set to pen:

> When we've been there [heaven] ten thousand years,
>    bright shining as the sun.
> We've no less days to sing God's praise
>    then when we'd first begun.

George Frederick Handel, popular opera-composer in England during the reign of King George III (the same king who refused to free the "colonies"), fell upon hard times. His operas were no longer popular, he was out of favor with the king, and he was desperate to find a new way to sustain himself. Presented with the opportunity to set to music the oratorio *The Messiah,* he went to work. Handel composed this lengthy and moving work in forty-three days. At the end, he was in total awe of the power of God and told friends that the Holy Spirit had guided his pen. Today we know it to be the most popular religious oratorio in the world. Yes, Handel was a believer, and had a deep love and respect for His Savior.

Johann Sebastian Bach, one of the greatest and certainly the most prolific classical composer who ever lived, was a devout Christian. He initialed at the upper left of each manuscript of a new composition he was working on, translated "Jesus help me!" At the end of the composition, after the last note he would initial, "For the glory of God!"

When King Solomon completed the building of the Temple in Jerusalem that King David had promised God, there would be a powerful demonstration of the Holy Spirit, *after* the musical presentation:

> And it came to pass, when the priests were come out of the holy place: (for all the priests that were present were sancti-

fied, and did not then wait by course: Also the Levites which were the singers, all of them of Asaph, of Heman, of Jeduthun, with their sons and their brethren, being arrayed in white linen, having cymbals and psalteries and harps, stood at the east end of the altar, and with them an hundred and twenty priests sounding with trumpets:) It came even to pass, as the trumpeters and singers were as one, to make one sound to be heard in praising and thanking the LORD; and when they lifted up their voice with the trumpets and cymbals and instruments of musick, and praised the LORD, saying, For he is good; for his mercy endureth for ever: that then the house was filled with a cloud, even the house of the LORD; So that the priests could not stand to minister by reason of the cloud: for the glory of the LORD had filled the house of God.

—2 Chronicles 5:11–14

How all of us who are connected with worship hope and pray for someday a similar visible outpouring of the Holy Spirit in our own worship service! Although I have never *seen* the Shekinah Glory appear, I *have* felt the presence of the Holy Spirit in such a powerful way that I, the singers and musicians, and the congregation were all reduced to awe and wonder — at a loss for words, followed by exuberant praises of our God and Savior. What a wonderful moment that is, but it *doesn't happen every Sunday,* nor can you "fake" the outpouring without damaging your own spiritual credibility.

Sadly, many worship directors try to make the Holy Spirit perform like a trained monkey. I have seen billboards guaranteeing a "miracle healing service!" We have *no right* to guarantee that the third person of the Trinity will show up and do our bidding. The same is true for those who knock down audiences with a wave of their hand, claiming that they have been knocked off their feet by the "Holy Spirit." Nothing could be further from the truth. Dressed in Armani suits, arriving by private jets and limousines, these televangelists *must* fake these manifestations to keep their power base alive, or they are coming from another source. Sadly, many of these spiritual hucksters use music, often credible praise songs and hymns, to prepare their audiences for their "show."

## Biblical Examples

And David and all Israel played before God with all their might, and with singing, and with harps, and with psalteries, and with timbrels, and with cymbals, and with trumpets.

—1 Chronicles 13:8

And the children of Israel that were present at Jerusalem kept the feast of unleavened bread seven days with great gladness: and the Levites and the priests praised the LORD day by day, singing with loud instruments unto the LORD.

—2 Chronicles 30:21

In Second Chronicles 20, the armies of the Ammonites and Moabites (today's Jordan) moved to attack Israel. The prophet Jahaziel told Israel not to be afraid of this approaching army because the battle was not theirs, but was God's! The prophet told King Jehosaphat to put his singers *in front* of Israel's army. Certain singers were to sing praises to the Lord, and to praise the beauty of His holiness. They went before the army of Israel, marching toward an overwhelming enemy singing:

Praise ye the LORD. O give thanks unto the LORD; for he is good: for his mercy endureth for ever. . . . O give thanks unto the LORD; for he is good: for his mercy endureth for ever.

—Psalm 106:1; 136:1

The result was that the attacking army, frightened and confused, turned on one another and began to fight amongst themselves. When the singers and the army of Israel (Judah) came to the place that overlooked the wilderness, they saw nothing but dead bodies — no one had escaped! Such is the power of music!

### Spiritual Power Through Music

In the many examples in the Bible about music and it's power, there are several common threads:

❖ The music is *always* directed toward God, celebrating His power, His goodness and His protection for those who have surrendered their lives to Him.

❖ The music is choral, not a pop solo singer with a back-up choir.

❖ The accompaniment is appropriate to the scene, celebration, praise, etc.

❖ No individual is singled out for performance praise.

❖ The lyrics are scriptural or liturgical — no "God is my buddy" nonsense.

❖ The music is always praise music, never celebrating individuals or their testimony.

❖ The music was not popular peasant "dance music" converted to spiritual use.

Again, the Bible is our guide, or should be our guide in *all things* related to worship. We can *never* go wrong if we use the Bible as our guide.

### Summary

There is awesome power in music. The power in spiritual music is magnified many times over the normal power of song. However, to truly be spiritual it has to be conceived by someone (a) walking with the Lord, (b) who writes the song for God, not for fame or profit, (c) who is willing to remain humble, and (d) who uses scripture and/or biblical principles as their guide.

Over and over throughout the Bible God tells us that He "sees" or reads our hearts. He knows when our motives are not pure. He knows when we frantically try to substitute an emotional experience for a spiritual experience. He knows when we begin to downplay Him and His word and upplay ourselves and the world system.

# How to Develop a Praise Band

Increasingly, congregations of mainline denominations are beginning to realize that to dedicate one regular religious service a week to a contemporary, informal, seeker-sensitive format with appropriate contemporary Christian music is a wise decision. This type of service appeals most to adolescents, young adults, and families that have not grown up in a church tradition. With the demise of music training in the public schools, the newer generations are often put off by the trappings of the formal church — including the music. A well-trained praise band, with professional leadership, an adequate budget, and support, is an essential part of this new format.

## What Is a Praise Band?

A contemporary praise band today usually consists of (a) three to six singers, (b) a rhythm section of drums, electric bass, synthesizers, and one or two guitars, and (c) an optional "horn line" of flute, sax, trumpet, or a full section.

The praise band had its historical roots in the modern black gospel movement of the 1920s and '30s, spearheaded by Thomas A. Dorsey. The instrumentation was not quite the same; this early modern black gospel music traditionally was accompanied by drums, electric bass (optional), Hammond B-3 organ, and a tenor sax.

In the 1960s, the Jesus Movement brought into the church contemporary pop and folk music — eventually leading to the Maranatha praise band format, a style of contemporary praise music most closely associated with Chuck Smith and the Calvary Church movement, headquartered in Costa Mesa, California. The Maranatha praise band instrumentation usually consists of two guitars, electric bass, drums, synthesizer, and three to six singers. Unison vocal lines, occasional harmonies, and occasional instrumental and vocal improvisation patterns are characteristic of this style. The Maranatha style has probably become the most successful model.

In the 1980s, two other formats began to appear. The first might be called the "Brooklyn Tabernacle" model. Utilizing a larger vocal ensemble, more elaborate arrangements, and more sophisticated harmonies, this model is exciting the Christian church and is highly appealing to singers and instrumentalists alike.

The other new format is a "jazz" format, either a combo with singer, *a la* Ella Fitzgerald, or singers and/or a big band behind a singer, *a la* Frank Sinatra. David Boyer (singer) and Ralph Carmichael (arranger) are probably the most positive role models for the Christian "big band" movement with solo singer. For the newest combo sound, the Cantos family is making a stir with their contemporary CDs and tapes, utilizing New Age, Latin, soft rock, and jazz influences. Brentwood Music is probably the recording and publishing company most caught up with the combo-jazz sound. Other influences on contemporary praise bands include Afro-Cuban music, contemporary Brazilian bossa-novas and sambas, calypso and reggae (Jamaican) styles.

## Statement of Philosphy

The purpose of the church has not changed: to reach the lost, to disciple them, to give them a spiritual community in which they can grow, and to meet the needs of the needy and oppressed. Styles of music come and go.

There is no spiritual "superiority" in the religious music of Europe versus the contemporary religious music of today. If there was, we should have all stayed with plain songs and Gregorian chants. I believe the well-rounded church must preserve, present, and protect the wonderful and inspiration musical traditions of the church that have developed over the past three hundred fifty years or more. On the other hand, the church has an obligation to bring into the church the best of the contemporary Christian music and present it with just as much conviction, staff, and budget as the traditional program requires to function at optimum level.

## Do You Really Want a Praise Band?

That's an honest question that many traditional churches cannot answer. Pressure from youth pastors, pressure from dropping attendance figures, pressure from local seeker-sensitive churches, pressure from mass media, records, radio, and television have forced many traditional churches to reluctantly introduce such a program — often without proper staff, budget, or commitment, usually guaranteeing failure, and getting the church off the hook with the statement, "Oh, well, we tried!"

Prayer and honesty are very important when beginning to trod down this path. A lot of soul-searching and open dialogue needs to take place. Often the traditional music staff feels threatened by the introduction of such a program and sometimes they will resist it — covertly or overtly.

Sometimes these stands against change take on cultural overtones, i.e., Rome's resistance to the creeping barbarian hordes from the north. An attitude of cultural superiority toward this "new" music will not and cannot lead to a healthy situation. Better the congregation hold off awhile until all have had a chance to discuss, pray, listen, and plan.

## Commitment

Starting a praise band is like a starting a new business. Most small businesses fail for one of two reasons: (a) the people running the business do not know what they are doing, or (b) the new business is undercapitalized. The same situation exists in starting a praise band. Make sure you know what you are doing, or hire someone that does — and be sure that you have committed enough budget and staff to make it happen.

## Training Program

I am a firm believer that not only do you have to create a new praise band out of your present resources, but you must at the same time begin a training program for future replacements and other bands. Failure to do so will leave you to the whims of chance regarding experienced personnel unless you hire professionals, as some churches are doing.

## Rehearsal Schedule

The praise band must meet at least two hours a week for a regular rehearsal. These rehearsals must be divided into the following major areas:

1. Proper warm-up
2. Preparation of music for the coming service
3. Training in new skills and solidifying the old
4. Going over new material
5. Record, play back, and analysis of at least one tune

## Sound Re-enforcement

Probably the most critical non-musical person assigned to work with this group is the sound engineer. He (or she) is vital in establishing proper balance, blend, and concept. Unlike the acoustic choir, organ, and piano, the praise band relies heavily on a proper mix of voices and instruments (as well as well-placed monitor speakers) for success. Please note that a training program is needed here as well.

### Concept

So much of developing a new musical style depends on concept. A wise former professor of mine once said, "No one can sing, play, conduct, compose, arrange, or teach beyond their own level of concept." How can an eskimo paint a palm tree if he's never seen one?

This is particularly true in developing the praise band. Money and time must be set aside for (a) buying and listening to quality CDs and videos, (b) attending concerts, (c) attending workshops, and (d) studying privately. Actually, more money needs to be spent here than on printed materials — at least in the beginning.

### Instruments

The good news is that most praise band personnel have their own instruments. You might need to invest in amplifiers and one or two synthesizers. Quality mikes are a must, along with some hand-held percussion, like tambourines, congas, etc.

### Recording

It is important to get a recording of the praise band into the hands of the congregation of the favorite (sung) praise songs. This can be a cassette recording done in-house. Use the DAT process for best quality and results.

### Mixed Signals

If you are going to do a contemporary service, do a contemporary service. Avoid mixing European traditional music, soloists, accompaniment styles, etc. You send a mixed message to the congregation. Allow your praise band to do your preludes, postludes, offertories, and communion music. Keyboard players can be trained quickly to do these things on a synthesizer. Most like the challenge.

### The Lyric
Read the lyrics, as a group, separate from the music. Highlight in yellow the most important words. Make the lyrics come alive. If you don't feel it, the congregation will not feel it either. Lyrics are everything in contemporary music! Put them first.

### Repetitive Songs
Be ready to change the accompaniment or the voice mix on strophic songs. Avoid doing three to five choruses of anything the same old way. Use solo voices, all men, all women, unison, two- or three-part harmony — whatever — to change things and make them more interesting.

### Melody and Bass Line
The melody and bass line are the two most important lines. They must balance. Everything else is secondary. Instrumentalists: avoid doubling the melody when it is being sung. It confuses the singer and takes away their ability to freely feel and phrase the music.

### Piano and Synthesizers
If you are using keyboards, try to have both of them playing synthesizers. The acoustic piano sends a mixed message and is difficult to blend in with the praise band sound. One keyboardist needs to be playing accompaniment patterns (comps, arpeggios, countermelodies, block chords) on an electric piano setting, preferrably a Fender-Rhodes sound. The other syn-

thesizer needs to be playing string or woodwind parts: block chords, high unison countermelody (two-octave parts), or special "punch" brass figures. Warning: One of the keys to a good sound in your praise band is getting your keyboard players working together.

## Guitars

If there is only one guitar, play rhythmic strums of the harmony, occasionally a single-note melody lead. If there are two guitars, one plays lead (or countermelody) while the other plays rhythm. One guitar is sufficient. Two creates problems until the players learn not to step on each others toes. Again, listening is critical here.

## Electric Bass

One of the key players in the group is the electric bass, which provides that big "bottom" that is so characteristic of contemporary music. The bass player must (a) play in tune, and (b) play in time. Out-of-tune bass players will make the whole group sound out of tune. Bass players who drag or rush create chronic rhythm anxiety in the group.

## Singers and Microphones

Singers: sing into the mike! Sing into the center of the mike! If you sing above or below, we lose tone and consonants. Think of the mike as a human ear. Move in close for intimate sounds, back away when opening up. Pop the consonants. Sing in the front part of the mouth. Since the PA system is building your tone and power, you can concentrate more on intonation, phrasing, and diction.

Watch your hands! Do something with them! Body language and facial expressions are very important here. Joyful, smiling singers really affect a congregation.

For country-western effects, tighten the lower jaw. For black gospel, move the tone back into the throat. For bright,

Broadway-show types of sound, sing in the very front of the mouth and behind the nasal cavities. Open up your mouths, particularly as you go (a) lower, (b) higher, or (c) louder.

## Volume

Watch the volume. Older people are particularly sensitive and put off by extremely loud music. Contemporary praise band music will be slightly louder than most acoustic groups. However, avoid extremely high volume levels. Remember, it's a religious service, not a concert.

## Costumes

I like to see a group that dresses with some type of uniform, even if it is informal. White shirts and blouses, Levis, white tennis shoes, etc., but get something uniform. If a praise band comes dressed in a wide variety of outfits, it visually suggests lack of precision, amateurism, etc. Believe me, it's worth the effort. People today are multisensory and must have eye-candy as well as ear-candy.

## Who's In Charge?

Too many chiefs and not enough Indians have spoiled many a church praise band. Someone must be in charge. This person must have spiritual as well as musical leadership and be respected by all. The music director must have the authority to speak with *authority.*

## Personnel

Spiritual maturity and reliability are the two most important prerequisites for membership in a praise band. Talent is important, but secondary. Avoid the temptation to put a talented but spiritually immature person in your praise band. Help them grow in the Lord first.

### Leading Worship vs. Performing

Always remind your group that they are not "performing." Artificial body language, smiles, gestures, and mike talk are not part of the praise band format. Please smile, be full of joy — but make it real.

### Sing to the Lord

Finally, make your voices and your instruments sing unto the Lord. I often pretend the Lord is sitting (sometimes with the disciples) in the front row of the balcony. I play for Him, I write for Him, I sing for Him, I live for Him!

If you want to "electrify" your services, do every musical number "as unto the Lord"!

# Music Literacy and the Church

Praise him with the sound of the trumpet: praise him with the psaltery and harp. Praise him with the timbrel and dance: praise him with stringed instruments and organs.

—Psalm 150:3–4

If you're going to praise God with all the instruments listed above, plus the singers, then some sort of music notation is required. Otherwise, it would take forever to teach by rote and memorize this kind of grand presentation to our Lord. That is why music literacy is so important to the future of church music, and why one of the main problems today in worship is the lack of music literacy.

### The Problem

Musical education has disappeared from today's public schools. Any attempt to teach the reading of music as a required academic discipline, or even as an elective, either departed long ago or was never a serious part of the school curriculum. Today, even private schools can usually afford only a minimal music program. Unfortunately, in most areas a private music conservatory system has not developed to replace the school programs.

Very few school systems in the United States have ever considered music an academic discipline, on the same plane as mathematics and science. This is unfortunate, because the Greek philosophers who contributed so much to the roots of our science and math concepts felt that music was equal to both. **In *The Republic,* Plato said in effect, "I care not what subject you teach, but let me teach music and I will control your society."** Today, we can say "amen" to that, as we watch the disc jockeys, MTV, and the record companies guide and direct our young musicians.

Even before the gradual erosion of music in America's schools, there has been a move away from music as a traditional discipline like mathematics and science, and a move toward music as a social recreational activity. Being musically literate long ago ceased to be a valid educational goal for a comprehensive curricula at any level.

For the first fifteen hundred years of church history, music was in the hands of professional musicians: organists and paid church choir members. An often forgotten goal of Martin Luther and the Protestant Reformation was that of allowing church congregations to participate in the music part of the worship service. To do this, they had to train their congregations (and their volunteer choirs) to *learn to read music.*

In Germany, even today, the government pays all expenses at the university level for students who major in law, medicine, or music. Germany believes these three areas of academic training are essential to their identity and the survival of their historical musical heritage. As a result, the state picks up the tab for the costs involved.

Most of today's pop (rock) entertainers are musically illiterate. They hire someone else to write down their songs and arrangements (or use a computer). This might account, in part, for the increasingly simplistic and childish melodies, harmonies, and arrangements we hear in today's music. Even a quick comparison of pop songs from the '40s and '50s like Nat King Cole's "Unforgettable" with any of say, Michael Jackson's big hits will graphically illustrate the decline of standards, taste, and excellence in pop music.

## The Impact

It is time for choir directors to wake up. Most of your congregations are musically illiterate. The decline in music literacy is already impacting church music programs. Soon, churches will not be able to offer the great major choral works of the past, like Handel's *Messiah* or Haydn's *The Creation*. It's virtually impossible to teach musical works of this size and magnitude by rote. What are we going to do for our Christmas and Easter celebrations, play tapes of the Mormon Tabernacle Choir?

As a result, in many Protestant churches today, music is back in the hands of the professionals. Even those not completely turning to professionals are salting their choirs with paid section leaders and hired-gun soloists for big concerts. Many have surrendered to the pressure from worldly parishioners who want to hear their praise songs presented in a rock band format. As a result, we are now seeing typical rock bands in church on Sundays. The only difference between what they do Saturday night in the local bar and what they do in the church on Sunday are the lyrics. As a result, it is increasingly more difficult to get into a worship mode with this type of music leading worship. What the church has done is to substitute worldly entertainment for traditional worship. This is not sitting well with many older and even younger but spiritually sensitive believers, but what to do?

## Why They Won't Sing?

People like to sing, but they do not want to make fools of themselves. It is one thing to hide out in the congregation, mumbling through hymns, hoping the person in front of you and next to you can't really hear you. It is another matter to stand in front of the congregation, with all eyes on you, and try to carry a tune. *Most churches could double the size of their choirs if they could provide an easy, painless, and quick method of learning how to read music.*

Also, the mumbling through a few hymns by the congregation, often accompanied by loud, out-of-tune, wobbly vocal amateurs, is less than inspiring and does little to elevate the praise and worship section of the service to the worshipful level desired. Young people in particular are turned off by most of what they see and hear in the way of inspirational church music in most of our churches today. You can't blame them for staying away when the music is poorly presented.

## The Answer

Start a music literacy program in your church. **Do it now**! Audio-visual aids, like the tape recorder and the VCR, now allow students to practice at home with professional instruction. Church-sponsored programs teaching vocal production and the basics of reading music are rapidly increasing. Intermediate and even advanced programs are found in some churches, giving singers the kind of solid training they need to stage excellent performances week after week.

I suggest starting an eight- to ten-week course, meeting once a week for ninety minutes, as the ideal program. At least two levels are needed, one for children from seven to thirteen years of age and another for those from fourteen years of age up to eighty. The best times for such a program seems to be late September through the middle of November and mid-January into March. Summer programs that begin in June and end no later than August 1 should also be considered.

The course should be divided into five parts:

a. Basic vocal technique (breathing, support, daily warm-up, tone, range, etc.)

b. Learning to read rhythms (meter, tempo, melodic, contrapuntal rhythms, etc.)

c. Learning to read melodies (solfeggio, moveable "do.")

d. Learning to sing in parts (monophonic to four-part)

e. Learning hymns, praise songs, and carols (some by rote, others by reading)

I have researched, written, and field-tested a music literacy training syllabus to help solve this problem. This syllabus has been used at the Village Presbyterian Church in Rancho Santa Fe, California, Calvary Church in Santa Ana, California (the largest church in the county), First Presbyterian in San Diego, and many other churches around the country. The textbook comes with a teaching guide, an audio tape package (that plays all the examples used in the text), and other helpful material.

Special rates for large orders are available. If you would like more information regarding this material, please write:

Music Literacy Training Program
% JCW Productions
Box 1331
Rancho Santa Fe, CA 92067

Besides my own program, there are many good, published music literacy programs now available. Those interested can contact me for a materials list. The other option is to develop your own customized program to fit the needs of your church and community.

## Community Benefits

Besides the benefit to the local church, a music literacy program opens up opportunities for all those participating to be able to transfer their skills to the study of other musical instruments, and is a general boost for school programs as well as community programs. Studies have shown that community music programs are one of the cheapest, fastest, and best ways of developing community pride, identity, and purpose.

## Financing the Program

I suggest a registration and materials fee of fifteen to twenty-five dollars, with scholarship money available for the children of needy families to participate. Most programs can be self-sustaining. Those requiring additional funds will place a minimal strain on the church music budget, and the investment will be well worth it. Class sizes should range from a minimum of five to a maximum of twenty-five.

## Don't Delay

The fact that the growing music illiteracy of our culture is *already* impacting church music programs places an urgency on introducing such a plan *as soon as possible*. As the family, the schools, and society as a whole, seem increasingly overwhelmed with today's problems, it seems increasingly appropriate for the church to step in where it can and lend a hand.

Classes can be scheduled back to back so that parents can participate as well. Child care is a consideration, if your class enrollments run high. Early evenings, Monday through Thursday, or Saturday mornings seem to be the best time. Some churches are running music literacy programs on Sunday mornings, allowing congregations to attend a service and then take a music literacy class before or after. I recommend surveying your congregation for the best times.

## The Instructor

The instructor must be capable of demonstrating and teaching basic vocal techniques, solfeggio, and eurhythmics. This person must be able to accompany and demonstrate musical examples on the piano (or guitar). Remember, enthusiasm is the number one prerequisite for good teaching!

# Rehearsal Techniques

Do all things without murmurings and disputings: That ye
may be blameless and harmless, the sons of God, without
rebuke, in the midst of a crooked and perverse nation, among
whom ye shine as lights in the world;

—Philippians 2:14–15

The greatness of any music conductor or leader is not what
the audience or congregation sees in performance. Great conductors and leaders are *rehearsal* experts. They know how to
make every moment count. They know where the difficult
passages are, they know how to drill on them, and they know
how to insure an accurate and enthusiastic performance.

This all takes a great deal of preparation. One of the common weaknesses of too many church music ensembles today
is that they are (a) not properly rehearsed, nor (b) have they
spent *enough time* rehearsing. The third part of this negative
trilogy would be (c) they tend to try to perform works too difficult for them.

The music director and the senior pastor *must* work carefully to select material that is appropriate for the church, the
sermon topic, the performing ensemble, and the congregation.
Again, I find too little time being spent in this area by too
many churches. Often the hymns and praise songs are select-

ed at random, at the last minute, and without careful consideration of their appropriateness and the ensemble's ability to prepare them properly.

For instance, most of the older hymns are in too high a key. They were written when people were smaller and their voices higher. As a result, the average parishioner cannot sing them comfortably. Lowering most of them one whole step will improve the congregational singing immediately.

"Winging" it on Sunday has become too common an occurrence. Some of this comes from the rock music world where last-minute spontaneity is substituted for musical discipline and preparation. Many of the top rock groups, like the Rolling Stones, do little or no preparation for recording an album, outside of selecting a theme and jotting down a few lyrics. The rest of it is worked out in the studio. That could work, if you're willing to spend a hundred hours or more in the recording studio to produce forty-five minutes of recorded music.

A professional rule of thumb is that there needs to be *one hour's rehearsal for each five to ten minutes of performed music.* That means that if your music ensemble or praise team are expected to present one half-hour of music on Sunday, they should have had *at least* three full hours of rehearsal preparation. Too often in church circles today, that is not the case. I know of one church that performs one half-hour of music on Sunday and rehearses for less than one hour, and that on Sunday morning, when corrections and outside polishing by singers and players is impossible. Even Leonard Bernstein, the great American composer and conductor could not produce musical excellence in this situation.

In many instances with these under-rehearsed, overly-performed ensembles they try to cover up by repeating the choruses of simple praise songs endlessly. This may charm some of the younger and less wise set in the congregation, but anyone with any musical sensitivity is irritated, outraged, and disappointed in what is obviously a musical con game. What a terrible emotional state to be in when trying to worship our Lord, who demands from each one of us that we do our *very best,* particularly when we are in worship. *Less is best* when there are time constraints.

Take some time to read some of the Old Testament prophets, like Hosea, Jeremiah, and Isaiah. There are some powerful passages in these books related to the Hebrews, who had grown jaded in their religious worship and were not offering their *best,* either in animals being presented for sacrifice or in their attitude or efforts.

Those who present these poorly prepared offerings to the living God should be quaking in their boots. As a professional musician, I could *never* perform, lead, or conduct under such conditions. As a believer in Christ, it is particularly repugnant to see standards that are so low that even talented amateur musicians are dismayed and distressed by the shoddy preparation. God demands our very best; anything less shows a lack of both respect and reverence for our Maker. If music directors, accompanists, singers, and musicians are not prepared to give their very best each and every Sunday, they should not be in music ministry. Simple is okay, if it is rehearsed properly, performed reverently, and is the very best that that particular music team is capable of producing.

As music director, you must be honest with your pastor and your ensemble. If you are asked to prepare a half-hour of music each Sunday and you neither have the time or the talent, you *must say so.* Quiet times of prayer between songs, scriptural readings, using more soloists — these are all good ways of covering the half-hour of music without taxing the talent of your group. If you have only one hour of rehearsal, then you can prepare only ten minutes (or less) of the worship part of the service. To try to do more insults the congregation and our Lord.

A great deal of thought and time should go into choosing the music for each Sunday. Balance is important. All contemporary praise songs of the same up-beat tempo begin to sound like a pep rally, not a worship service. The old and the new must be represented. Old favorite hymns must be sung as well, but *with respect.* I'm still recovering from having heard "A Mighty Fortress Is Our God" performed to a poorly-performed, too-loud rock style accompaniment, with a young, poorly-trained (even by rock standards) drummer who played a *heavy* rock dance beat to this most sacred of Christian hymns. It was the worst kind of culture shock and made worship almost an impossibility. On top of it, the drummer and his companions were dressed like they had just come from working on their cars in the backyard: wrinkled Levis, soiled t-shirts, and stained Nike jogging shoes.

How and why congregations put up with this sort of thing is beyond me. It's as though everyone must look the other way, otherwise we might offend one of our younger church attendees. They *need* direction, higher standards, and something to *work toward.* They also need to know that being part of a worship team is *serious* business and should not be taken lightly. It probably is the *most* important thing in their life and should be considered an *honor,* not an obligation. Where is the music director? Where is the pastor? Where are the elders and deacons of the church?

## Basic Guidelines

Basic guidelines in choosing appropriate material would include (a) appropriateness of the lyrics, (b) tempo and style, (c) level of difficulty, (d) appropriateness for the sermon topic, (e) appropriateness for the season, (f) appropriateness for the congregation, and (g) within the talent and time constraints imposed on the music team.

More careful attention needs to be paid to the lyrics of the songs being sung in church today. Many lyrics are either pop "love" ballads with the name "Jesus" substituted for "baby," or they suggest a palsy-walsy intimacy with the Creator of the universe that is neither scriptural nor worshipful. Others are what I call "bumper-sticker" songs — songs with no content, except for a single phrase, like "I love Jesus," or "man, what a guy!" These songs not only insult the intelligence of the listeners, they degrade the worship service into a kind of groovy Hollywood "roast" for our favorite guy — Jesus! The ultimate "dumbing-down" of the gospel message.

The most important part of the musical message is the lyrics. Too often, neither the director nor the singers truly understand the over-all message and meaning of the song. I always had my vocal groups *read* the lyrics, sometimes several times, before we sang them. Ask questions like: (a) "What's the primary meaning of this song or hymn?" or (b) "What prompted the composer to write it?" or (c) "What's the *key* word or phrase in the song?" and finally, (d) "What emotion or emotions should we (the singers) feel and then convey to the congregation when we sing this song?"

Often I would stop in the middle of a final run-through and ask different singers to tell me (a) what they were feeling at that moment, and (b) what was the lyric saying at that particular spot. Too often, lyrics are sung like reading the want-ads in a newspaper. Remember, if we, the performers, do not feel or understand the song *neither will the congregation.*

There is an ancient graffiti carved into the backstage area of the large Greek amphitheater in Ephesus, Turkey. It must have been written by an ancient actor or musician between scenes. Roughly translated it says, "If *you* [the actor or musician] don't feel it [the emotion], *they* [the audience or congregation] will not feel it either!" You can't fake it or pretend. The audience (or congregation) will find you out. To have a convincing performance, there is no way out. You, the performer *must* feel *intensely* the message you are presenting or it's all a waste of time. Even musical excellence will not make up for lack of feeling when presenting your hymns, songs and choruses.

Several years ago, *Psychology Today* did a major study of the impact of singers on an audience. This was a detailed study and was confirmed by other research in later studies. Their findings were startling:

❖ Fifty-five percent of the impact of any musical performance is the *body language* of the performer or performers (assuming they are singers).
❖ The next twenty-five percent was the impact of the delivery of the lyric of the song (or hymn).
❖ The last twenty percent was the musical skill and presentation offered.

Very revealing. Our body sends the most *powerful* message, our understanding and delivery of the lyric is next, and last is our musical skills! Unfortunately, in many churches, these priorities are reversed.

In most churches today little or no time is spent on body language, then next to nothing on the deeper meaning of the lyrics. The lion's share of the rehearsal time is spent polishing the music. No wonder we have multi-millionaire singer/songwriters in pop music today who's musical skills are limited, but who's body language and lyric delivery are outstanding and who are always capable of getting a rousing response from their audience.

I would always record my last run-through in rehearsal and then have my singers lip-sync the lyrics in front of a full-length mirror. I can't tell you the impact this innovation in rehearsal had on the performances in our worship services! Don't skip it, it's a must!

The next most important thing is the *melodies*. Melodies must be sung *in tune* and *in time*. Again, I would always tell my singers and musicians, "If it isn't in tune and in time it isn't music — it's noise!" Because of the lack of standards in popular music since the 1960s many millionaire rock musicians have yet to sing in tune or in time. This lowering of musical standards has rubbed off on church musicians. That shouldn't happen.

Those of us in church music must march to a different drummer. We have a different standard and we should accept *no compromise* in this area. If you have a singer or singers who can't handle these two qualifications, ask them kindly but firmly to seek the Lord for another way to serve Him in church work. If they persist, insist on private lessons and/or a course in ear training from the local community college or adult high school program. Bad singers and musicians will eventually drive away good singers and players. *Don't take the chance.* Keep the standards high!

Good balance is *demanding* that the lyric and melody *always* are heard above the accompaniment. Again, this is too often not the case in the pop-rock music world, where the accompaniment often drowns out the singer, so he or she has to "shout" to be heard. This is musical chaos and *does not belong in the church.* Tell your accompanists and musicians that any time they cannot hear the lyrics and the melody, *they are playing too loudly.* Stop often in rehearsals when this occurs. *Insist* on good balance.

Every musical selection has it's own *correct* tempo. If the tempo, or speed is too fast, the lyrics are jumbled together and cannot be understood. If the tempo is too slow, the musical phrases and sentences fall apart and the meaning of the song disappears. Be very sensitive to tempo. Experiment with taking the selection a bit faster or slower — ask your singers to help you find the *right* tempo. Also, remember that when we are on stage and under performance pressure we tend to take everything *too fast*. Music director's should "think" through the first phrase of each tune to find the correct tempo before giving the downbeat to your singers and musicians.

A standard criticism of rock music is the constant loudness of the tempo. It's like a room full of people where everyone is shouting at the top of their voice. This may create excitement and emphasize the rebelliousness of rock music, but it wreaks havoc in a worship service. The single greatest criticism leveled at contemporary Christian music when it is introduced into the church is that it is *too loud*. Please re-read the fight-or-flight chapter in this book, or read it to your musicians.

Loud music stimulates *anger, aggression, and uncontrollable behavior*. That excitement is being substituted today in many church's for true worship. Nerve excitement is just that; worship is something different. *Tone it down*. If you must use a drummer in your praise band, take away his sticks and give him brushes — except for the special numbers. Remember, the primary reason rock music is so loud is so that it will trigger the fight-or-flight response, producing uncontrolled aggressiveness and extreme emotional reactions to the music. Do we really want this in our churches today?

All great art is based on contrast. Too much unity — boredom. Too much variety — chaos. Try to look for opportunities to make your songs more interesting by:

* Using sudden changes in dynamics (loud-soft)
* Dropping out the accompaniment and singing accappella (unaccompanied)
* Using just female, or male voices
* Introducing instrumental solo interludes (piano, flute, etc.)
* Cutting the tempo in half, or doubling up on the tempo
* Gradually slow down or speed up or get softer or louder.

Record your last run-through in rehearsal and allow time to play it back to your singers and players. Too many church ensembles have never heard themselves as the congregation hears them. I have found that this technique is the single *most important* teaching tool I have ever discovered for improving a musical performance. I would ask my groups, "Is this (the recorded run-through) good enough to sell in the local record store? If not why not?" Believe me, the time you take to do this is well spent.

## Summary

Finally, listen to outstanding groups on CDs, videos, live concerts, and local rehearsals. Study body language, lyric interpretation, pacing of the program, all the things that make that group or soloist *outstanding*.

Water cannot rise above its own level. No musician can compose, conduct, lead, or perform beyond their own level of concept. This conceptual level can only be stretched by exposing yourself and your musicians to the very best musical experiences available in their particular genre of music.

Ask the Lord to help you. Be humble enough to ask for advice from your singers and musicians, the congregation, other directors, etc. The Lord will help you — as will others — if you are humble enough to accept the help. Remember, in the Bible, *pride* is the number one sin and *humility* is the number one virtue. When I was a lad, I used to have a private music instructor who would write above my assignment sheet each lesson, "It's what you learn after you know it all that counts!" I wonder what he meant by that?

> Let nothing be done through strife or vainglory; but in lowliness of mind let each esteem other better than themselves. Look not every man on his own things, but every man also on the things of others.
>
> —Phillipians 2:3–4

# Check List for Music Directors

And when those beasts give glory and honour and thanks to him that sat on the throne, who liveth for ever and ever, The four and twenty elders fall down before him that sat on the throne, and worship him that liveth for ever and ever, and cast their crowns before the throne, saying, Thou art worthy, O Lord, to receive glory and honour and power: for thou hast created all things, and for thy pleasure they are and were created.

—Revelation 4:9–11

Below are twenty-five suggestions to church music directors covering everything from inventory to music and spiritual development. This list is also a good checklist for church administrators to use in the annual evaluation of their chief music director, or as questions to ask an applicant for an open position as minister or director of music.

## Check List

1. Inventory of all music, instruments, and equipment. Regular maintenance of pianos, organs annually. Figure yearly depreciation and set aside funds for future replacements.
2. Work to develop professional quality vocal production, tone,

phrasing, concept. Breathing exercises, warm-up exercises, range, intonation, diction, enunciation, and tonal exercises are a must for developing your singers. Don't assume knowledge or background — teach it! The human voice is the most delicate of all instruments and must be trained and maintained properly.

3. Select major works for Easter, Mother's Day, Father's Day, Memorial Day, Fourth of July, Thanksgiving, and Christmas *early*. Do *not* try to perform works that would be over the head of your singers and musicians. One of the first negative characteristics of an amateur ensemble is their tendency to perform musical selections too difficult for their group. Look for opportunities to perform special (new) music arranged or composed *specifically* for your group.

4. Prepare an annual music budget. Look for opportunities to borrow or rent more expensive works. Include sing-along CDs to help train your group faster.

5. Survey your congregation at least *twice* a year. Ask them to tell you what they like and what they don't like about the music. Ask them to list their favorite hymns and choruses. Ask them to name their favorite religious work (*The Messiah,* etc) as well as their favorite Christian CD. Look for musicians and singers in your congregation by asking in the survey for: (a) previous musical experience, (b) interest in singing or playing in the ensemble, (c) interest in attending a music literacy training program, or (d) joining a drama team.

6. Work with pastors to find appropriate music for sermon topics. This is a *must*. Try to work at least six weeks in advance. It's okay if the pastor switches sermon topics, but he *must* let you know in time to find appropriate music.

7. If you are in a large, traditional church your position will require you to supervise and/or train a chancel choir, youth

choir, children's choir, men's glee, women's glee, praise band, quartets, soloists, and bell choir. Today, in many instances, your primary responsibility will be to train the praise band and singers and line up soloists for the offertory and special music. Don't forget to start a youth training program so you have a feeder group into your primary ensemble.

8. Develop a regular music literacy training program for seniors and juniors. This is a *must*, unless you are willing to forget all the major choral works, old and new, that have been written for the church.

9. Develop, train, and arrange for a contemporary praise band. One of the best training programs available for this is the Maranatha Praise Band Training Program. Maranatha also does workshops around the country for music leaders.

10. Record a CD of your church's most popular praise songs. Make the CD available to the congregation for a nominal fee. Many parishioners would sing more enthusiastically if they could practice singing along with the music at home or in the car during the week. Use the extra funds raised from this project for special needs in the music department; i.e., equipment, music, attending workshops, touring, or recording.

11. Work with soloists. Preview all solo performances *before* church services. Edit, alter, or delete all questionable selections, accompaniment style, length of performance, etc.

12. Contact the local musician's union for paid professionals for special events and works.

13. Attend workshops, belong to professional groups, seek additional training *regularly*, i.e., Choral Directors Guild.

14. Make contact with other local churches. Arrange for an exchange of music teams occasionally on Sunday, or combine for special events.

15. Get to know and work closely with the chairperson of the

music committee for your church (if you have one). Discuss differences, needs, and long-range planning.

16. Help with special music for summer Bible camp, church retreats, and workshops.

17. If possible, pre-record a rehearsal tape, particularly for the singers, at least one week before each service. This will help immensely in allowing each singer to gain familiarity with the songs *before* they are performed. If that's not possible, have each singer bring a tape recorder to rehearsal so they can tape the songs for themselves.

18. Schedule an annual church talent night. Use it as a fundraiser. Encourage *anyone* from the congregation who can dance, sing, play a musical instrument, be a comedian, or a mime to participate. Content does not have to be religious.

19. Encourage at least one annual evening hymn and chorus sing-a-long, where favorite hymns and choruses are sung by soloists, the praise ensemble, the choir, and the congregation. Keep it simple, keep it moving.

20. Look for opportunities to work with other churches, church schools, well-known soloists, etc. Combine with other churches to perform major works too challenging for your church alone. This will inspire and motivate your musicians and singers.

21. Let your praise band and/or choir and singers have at least four to six weeks off during late summer. Use guest soloists, small groups, youth groups, etc.

22. Start the fall season with a music group retreat or workshop. Bring in a guest clinician if you can. Invite new members. Make it social, make it fun.

23. Lay out an annual calendar, beginning in September through June or July. Include the dates for special performances, concerts, extra rehearsals, tours, and workshops.

24. Take time to meet, talk, and pray with each member of

your group. Stress the importance (to them) of this ministry. Tell them, that according to Old Testament traditions, they are "Levites," they are from the priestly class, and God sees them as being just as important as the pastors, elders and deacons.

25. Submit yourself and the members of your ensemble to the power and the will of the Almighty God. Do not participate in this ministry if you or any member of your group is participating in willful and unconfessed sin or are not convinced that Jesus Christ was and is God in the flesh and we are His servants.

## Summary

Although not totally comprehensive, this list is a good place to start as a measuring tool for a well run music program in a church. Other ideas and adaptations for your particular situation should be added as seen fit. But *keep your standards high.* You are preparing a worship service, not for yourself, your pastor, the elder board, or the congregation. You are preparing a worship service for the King of Kings and Lord of Lords. The primary ingredient for success in music ministry is a true sense of humility, wonder, and awe as you prepare music each week for the Creator of the universe and a willingness to not only *take but to seek objective criticism as well as a constant drive to do better each and every week. Don't ever take your position for granted. Believe me, God doesn't.

> And they sung a new song, saying, Thou art worthy to take the book, and to open the seals thereof: for thou wast slain, and hast redeemed us to God by thy blood out of every kindred, and tongue, and people, and nation; And hast made us unto our God kings and priests: and we shall reign on the earth.
>
> —Revelation 5:9–10

# Summary

Blessed are they that keep judgment, and he that doeth righteousness at all times.

—Psalm 106:3

The crisis in Christian music is part of a bigger problem in America. The dumbing down of our culture began in the 1960s, and it has permeated all the arts and eventually seeped into church music. Nerve excitement and the discovery that music could be used as a drug by rock musicians soon began to be accepted as a demonstration of an outbreak of the Holy Spirit in the church, instead of what it really was, an artificial stimulation of the fight-or flight response that produced a dangerous emotional high.

The post-World War II birth of existentialism (Jean Paul Sartre) as a modern philosophy, where the only moral guidelines were those that were self-imposed, leaked into theology, leading to a weakened church, with a Savior who looked and seemed more like a suntanned surfer than the God of the universe in the flesh. As a result, the worship songs became more friendly and, "Hi, how are ya?" than letting us feel the power and the glory of an almighty God.

The disappearance of music literacy from our school curriculums eventually spelled doom for most large church choirs, since an increasing number of church attendees could not read music. As a result, watered-down rock bands accompany unison singers singing nursery rhyme simple songs to a congregation that has already, for the most part, accepted this as just another example of the dumbing down of our culture.

The new model of the "seeker-sensitive" churches, particularly in the urban areas surrounding large cities in America, has also contributed to the problem. The philosophy of the seeker-sensitive church in trying to be a bridge between the secular and the sacred worlds may have gone too far in casualness and world-influenced music. These churches seek to entertain and serve as social service centers in helping lonely urbanites make contact with each other. That's nice, but is it the primary purpose of the church? Many of these churches have stopped singing or performing traditional Christian hymns and choruses because their surveys indicate that the non-believer does not "like" that kind of music.

Could it be that the powerful spiritual message of many of the great hymns and choruses bring the non-believer under conviction? That's the purpose of the gospel and gospel music, not to entertain, but to uplift the believer and to bring the non-believer under conviction. "Liking" the music is not the issue here. Pleasing God, being obedient to His will, and worshipping Him in an appropriate manner, *regardless* of the attitudes of the non-believer is our job, not to entertain, cajole, and tickle under the chin the non-believer with an apologetic, watered-down musical and pastoral message.

I'm not sure backing into the essential message of the gospel — that we are all sinners and unless we declare Jesus Christ as our Lord and Savior (John 3) we are doomed to hell for eternity — to avoid "offending" the non-believer is the right approach. Neither do I approve of hitting non-believers over their heads with our Bible. However, once you compromise the integrity of the gospel, the true purpose of worship and the primary message of salvation, where do you stop?

Even with these changes there is still no excuse for the kind of slovenly, poorly-prepared, poorly-performed worship music heard too often today in our churches. Even the simplest of musical ensembles can still have high standards and not perform anything that is not properly rehearsed or that is technically beyond that particular group's ability.

This book has attempted to 1) identify the problem, 2) explain how it got this way, and 3) offer some positive suggestions on how to improve the situation. Not all contemporary Christian music is "bad." Not all traditional church music is "good." However, there has been a weakness in bringing contemporary Christian music (meant to be an evangelical outreach to lost teenagers) into the sanctuary as acceptable praise music for a worship service. In most instances, there is not a comfortable transfer from one purpose and media of performance to another.

Another purpose of the book has been to alert the reader to the awesome *power* of music. In fact, this author is also working on a larger, more comprehensive book that will take at least a year to research, *The Power of Music,* a book that will in detail explore the physiological, emotional, cultural, spiritual, and social aspects of music in modern-day culture.

## Danger!

Recently a car pulled up next to mine, and the music the driver was listening to was so loud that the entire car vibrated. On this car was a bumper sticker which read, *"If It's Too Loud, You're Too Old."* That might be so, but if it's that loud, the listener is in danger of a) burning out their adrenal glands through overactivating of the fight-or-flight response, b) damaging their mid-range hearing beyond repair, and c) getting hooked on music as a drug, with the same dangers that any recreational drug use offers today, with the exception of incarceration.

Pastors, music leaders, elders, and deacons, need to all work together to cut across generation lines in defining an appropriate and worshipful policy for music in their church. Failure to do so will continue to divide congregations and will continue the trend where today churches are more defined by the nature and quality of their music than by any other standard: pastor, denomination, physical facilities, etc.

## Attack!

Satan throughout history has *always* attacked the church. He fears the church, for he knows that strong, biblically literate Christians who know the *real* purpose of worship (driving out the forces of darkness) will cause more damage to his kingdom than any other method. Since the battlefield is the mind, and music has an incredible and powerful affect on the mind (and the emotions) it is no wonder that he has chosen music as his *primary* and most effective way to compromise the power and spiritual integrity of the modern church.

As believers and church members, we *must* understand this and be ready for his onslaught. Taking demonized music and writing Christian lyrics for it, is the kind of compromise that plays right into his hands, because he *knows* that music and how it is presented can overpower a weak Christian lyric and plant the *wrong* seed in the mind and emotions of the believer.

> But the fruit of the Spirit is love, joy, peace, longsuffering, gentleness, goodness, faith, Meekness, temperance: against such there is no law.
>
> —Galatians 5:22,23

Our music in the church should reflect and identify with the fruits of the spirit. If the music does not, it does not belong in the sanctuary. On the other hand:

> Now the works of the flesh are manifest, which are these; Adultery, fornication, uncleanness, lasciviousness, Idolatry, witchcraft, hatred, variance, emulations, wrath, strife, seditions, heresies, Envyings, murders, drunkenness, revellings, and such like: of the which I tell you before, as I have also told you in time past, that they which do such things shall not inherit the kingdom of God.
>
> —Galatians 5:19–21

## Rebellion

The battle cry of rock music was and is: *Sex, Drugs, and Rock 'n Roll!* A fourth cry would be *rebellion*. Samuel told King Saul that God sees rebellion as *idolatry*. Do we really think we can take this kind of music into the church, clean up the lyrics, and sell it as "spiritual" music? I think not. I also think that we make a mistake by being too eager to bring the world into the church, and not eager enough to take the church out into the world.

> Love not the world, neither the things that are in the world. If any man love the world, the love of the Father is not in him. For all that is in the world, the lust of the flesh, and the lust of the eyes, and the pride of life, is not of the Father, but is of the world.
>
> 1 John 2:15–16

The world is Satan's turf. He understands it, he controls it. To try to use the music of *his* world to attract potential new believers to *Jesus'* world will not work. If it had, Paul the apostle would have brought the music of Corinth into the Corinthian church, if it wasn't there already.

## A Higher Standard

The Bible says that God holds those who preach and teach to a higher standard. As already discovered in earlier chapters in this book, the Jews considered musicians to be priests, and they were required to come from the tribe of Levi and be trained in the same way. Paul the apostle said that he worked out his salvation with "fear and trembling." I believe that fear was the awesome responsibility of teaching and defending the gospel. I believe that the music we choose for worship and how we present it is every bit as important in God's eyes as the pastor's sermon, maybe more important, since the Bible shows us (Rev. 4–5) that we will be "worshipping" in heaven, but not necessarily listening to long sermons.

The early church had to rely on the Holy Spirit. Much prayer was devoted to being in tune with the "Comforter" which Jesus said He would send (John 14), a Comforter that would teach us *all things.* I also believe today's church is too busy aping the techniques of the modern business world and not attentive enough to the voice of the Holy Spirit. After all, it is God, not man, that built the church. Let's all listen more closely to His voice and less to those who sell modern Christianity as if it were a commercial product.

As long as we are in tune with Jesus and not with the world, the Holy Spirit will guide us and teach us *all things.* However, for that to happen, we have to be more sensitive to His voice than to the siren's call of the world. Music is a bridge between earth and heaven. It is also a bridge between earth and hell. Just be careful which bridge you take, or lead others on.

> But the Comforter, which is the Holy Ghost, whom the Father will send in my name, he shall teach you all things, and bring all things to your remembrance, whatsoever I have said unto you.
>
> —John 14:26

I am the vine, ye are the branches: He that abideth in me, and I in him, the same bringeth forth much fruit: for without me *ye can do nothing*.

—John 15:5

If ye were of the world, the world would love his own: but because ye are not of the world, but I have chosen you out of the world, therefore the world hateth you.

—John 15:19

## Love Not the World

Does the world hate the church in America? In most instances, not really. In fact, we can hardly wait to cuddle up closer to Satan's kingdom rather than God's. The gospel, and the music accompanying it, is a two-edged sword: it feeds the believer, attracts the unsaved, and angers the sinner. Does the choice of your music "anger" the sinners in your congregation? If so, rejoice, you're on the right track!

*Appendix A*

# Arranging for Praise Bands and Modern Choirs

## Choices

voices, strings, brass, woodwinds, percussion, keyboards (synthesizer, ethnic)

## Ranges

### High

soprano voice, violin, whistling, piccolo, flute (high register), harmonica, oboe, soprano sax, alto sax (high register), clarinet (high register), trumpet (high register), flugel horn (high register), xylophone, bells

### Medium

alto voice, tenor voice (high register), violin, viola, cello (high register), clarinet (medium/low register), alto sax, flute (low register), alto flute (normal), English horn, harmonica, trumpet, flugel horn, French horn, trombone (high register), guitar (high register)

### Medium-Low

tenor voice (low register), baritone voice, bass voice (high register), viola (low register), cello bass viol (high register), guitar, bass flute, clarinet (low register), bassoon, bass clarinet (high register), tenor sax, baritone sax, trombone, bass trombone, tuba (high register)

### *Low*
cello (low register), bass viol, bass clarinet (low register), bassoon (low register), bass trombone, tuba, electric bass, tuned percussion

### *All Registers*
harp, piano, synthesizer, organ, ethnic (Kalimba)

## Assignment of Parts
Melody (must always be prominent)
Countermelody (next in importance)
Bass line (third most important line)
Rhythmic "comp" patterns
Sustained harmonic background
Percussion

## Basic Do's and Don'ts
Avoid writing in the extreme registers (high or low).
Avoid using similar-range instruments against voices.
Write less. Every note must mean something.
Keep it simple. Avoid complex rhythmic or harmonic patterns.
Observe the unity-variety principle.
When in doubt, use a successful model.
Rhythm is *always* the most important element in music.
Interior lines should move as smoothly as possible.
Don't throw everything you know into an arrangement.
Less is always better.
Don't change moods, styles, tone color, or register in midstream.
Balance unity (sameness) with variety (new ideas).

### References

*Harmony, Counterpoint, and Orchestration* books by Walter Piston

*Modern Arranging* books by Henry Mancini, Nelson Riddle, Russ Garcia, and Sammy Nestico

*Arranging for Today's Church Choir* by Jack Wheaton

*Electronic Orchestration, Composing for Films, Layout Technique* and *101 Compositional Ideas* (books or pamphlets) by Jack Wheaton

*Keyboard Magazine*

*Electronic Musician*

# Recommended Praise Songs

The following list is not a comprehensive list of acceptable praise songs. It will, however, give you some guidelines in selecting suitable material for your church or group.

The criteria for selection includes the following:

* Scriptural or inspirational message based upon fundamental Christian teachings.
* Modern but not overly syncopated or repetitive rhythms.
* Melodic intervals compliment the lyrics and deepen their meaning.
* Form is not too repetitive; good balance between unity and variety.
* Harmonic progressions complimentary to lyrics and appropriate for the song.
* Easy-to-remember message, easy-to-remember melody.

Warning: Any of these selections can be turned into an unacceptable presentation due to (a) too much volume, (b) too much repetition, (c) inappropriate arrangement, or (d) too much added syncopation or improvisation.

*Alleluiah* (Rev. 19:12)
*Amazing Love* — Graham Kendrick
*As the Deer* (Ps. 42:8) — Martin Nystrom

*Be Exalted, O God* (Ps. 57:10–11) — Brent Chambers
*Because He Lives* (John 14:19) — Bill Gaither
*Bind Us Together* (John 17:20–21) — Bob Gillman
*Bless His Holy Name* (Ps. 103:1) — Andrae Crouch

*Cares Chorus* (1 Pet. 5:7) — Kelly Willard
*Change My Heart, Oh God* (Ps. 51:10) — Eddie Espinosa
*Come Let Us Worship and Bow Down* (Ps. 95:6–7) — Dave
    Doherty
*Create in Me a Clean Heart* (Ps. 51) — Author Unknown

*Emmanuel* (Isa. 7:14) — Bob McGee

*Give Thanks with a Grateful Heart* (Ps. 126:3) — Henry Smith
*Glorify Thy Name* (John 12:28) — Donna Adkins
*Great Is the Lord* (Jer. 32:17) — Michael and Deborah Smith

*He Has Made Me Glad* (Ps. 100:4;118:24) — Leona Von
    Brethorst
*He Is Lord* (Phil. 2:9–11) — Tom Fettke
*His Name Is Wonderful* (1 Cor. 12:3) — Audrey Mieir
*Hosanna* (Ps. 118) — Carl Tuttle
*How Majestic Is Your Name* (Ps. 8:1) — Michael W. Smith

*I Exalt Thee* (Ps. 97:9) — Pete Sanchex, Jr.
*I Love You, Lord* (2 Chron. 6:40) — Laurie Klein
*I Will Call Upon the Lord* (Ps. 18:3) — Michael O'Shields
*I Will Sing of the Mercies* (Ps. 89:1) — James H. Fillmore
*In Moments Like These* — David Graham

*Jesus, Name All Names* (2 Thess. 1:12) — Naida Hearn

*Majesty, Worship His Majesty* — Jack Hayford
*Make Me a Servant* (Matt. 20:26) — Kelly Willard

*O, How I Love Jesus* (2 Pet. 1:8) — Fredrick Whitfield
*O Lord, You're Beautiful* (Ps. 34:15) — Keith Green
*Oh, How He Loves You and Me* — Kurt Kaiser
*On Eagle's Wings* — Michael Joncas
*Open Our Eyes, Lord* (Matt. 5:8) — Robert Culli
*Our God Reigns* (Isa. 52:7) — Leonard W. Smith, Jr.

*Priase the Name of Jesus* (1 Cor. 10:4) — Roy Hicks

*Shine, Jesus, Shine* (John 12:46) — Graham Kendrick
*Sing Alleluiah to the Lord* (Ps. 84:2) — Linda Stassen

*The Greatest Thing* — Mark Pendergrass
*This Is the Day* (Ps. 118:24) — Les Garrett
*Thou Art Worthy* (Rev. 4:11) — Pauline M. Mills
*Thy Loving Kindness* (Ps. 63) — Hugh Mitchell
*Thy Word* (Ps. 119:9) — Michael W. Smith

*We Are God's People* (2 Pet. 2:9) — based on the finale to
    Brahm's Symphony No. 1
*White As Snow* — Leon Olguin
*Worthy Is the Lamb* (Rev. 5:12) — Don Wyrtzen

*You Are My Hiding Place* (Ps. 31:19–20) — Michael Ledner

# Most Popular Praise Songs
# for 1999

According to a detailed survey by Maranatha Music, based on data from copyright licensing and other sources, the following are the most popular praise songs for the year:

- ❖ All Hail King Jesus
- ❖ As the Deer
- ❖ Awesome God
- ❖ Because He Lives
- ❖ Celebrate Jesus
- ❖ Change My Heart, O God
- ❖ Give Thanks
- ❖ Glorify Thy Name
- ❖ Great Is the Lord
- ❖ He Has Made Me Glad (I Will Enter His Gates)
- ❖ He Is Exalted
- ❖ Holy Ground
- ❖ How Majestic Is Thy Name
- ❖ I Exalt Thee
- ❖ I Love you, Lord

❖ Jesus, Name Above All Names
❖ Lord I Lift Your Name on High
❖ Majesty
❖ More Precious Than Silver
❖ O Magnify the Lord (I Will Call Upon the Lord)
❖ Open Our Eyes
❖ Shine, Jesus, Shine (Lord, the Light of Your Love)
❖ Shout to the Lord
❖ This Is the Day
❖ We Bring the Sacrifice of Praise

Some of the songwriters of this year's most popular praise songs include Rick Founds, Darlene Zschech, Jack Hayford, Rich Mullins, Graham Kendrick, Michael W. Smith, and Twila Paris.

# Bibliography

### Books

*All God's Children and Blue Suede Shoes: Christian and Popular Culture* (Westchester, IL: Crossway Books, 1989).

Baker, Paul, *Why Should the Devil Have All the Good Music?* (Waco, TX: Word Books, 1979).

Benson, Carl, ed., *The Bob Dylan Companion* (Schirmer Books, 1998).

Best, Harold, *Music and the Church: A Theology of Church Music* (Nashville, TN: Broadman Press, 1989).

Booth, Stanley, *Keith* (of the Rolling Stones) (New York: St. Martin's Press, 1995).

Broadbent, E. H., *Pilgrim Church* (Grand Rapids, MI: Gospel Folio Press, 1933, rev. 1999).

Broughton, Dimon, Mark Ellingham, David Muddymand, and Richart Trillo, *The Rough Guide to World Music* (London: Penguin Books, 1994).

Colson, Chuck, *The Body* (Dallas: Word Books, 1992).

Edwards, Jonathan, *Sinners in the Hands of an Angry God* (New Kensington, PA: Whitaker House, 1997).

Graham, Billy, *Just As I Am* (New York: Harper/Collins, 1997).

Green, Melody and David Hazard, *No Compromise* (Nashville, TN: Sparrow Press, 1989).

Hanegraaff, Hank, *Counterfeit Revival* (Dallas: Word Books, 1997).

Hayford, Jack W., *Worship His Majesty* (Waco, TX: Word Books, 1987).

*The Hole in Our Soul: The Loss of Beauty and Meaning in American Popular Music* (New York: Free Press, 1997).

Joseph, Mark, *Rock and Roll Rebellion* (Nashville, TN: Broadman & Holman Pub., 1999).

*Learning to Worship as a Way of Life* (Minneapolis, MN: Bethany House, 1984).

Leisch, Barry, *The New Worship* (Grand Rapids, MI: Baker Books, 1996).

Lewish, C. S., *The Business of Heaven* (New York: Harvest House/ HBJ, 1984).

Medved, Michael, *Hollywood vs. America* (New York: Harper/Collins, 1992).

Morgenthaler, Sally, *Worship Evangelism* (Grand Rapids, MI: Zondervan, 1995).

*Music Through the Eyes of Faith* (San Francisco: Harper, 1993).

Noebel, David, *Hypnotism and the Beatles: The Legacy of John Lennon*

----------, *Rhythm, Riots, and Revolution*

Osbeck, Kenneth W., *101 Hymn Stories* (Grand Rapids, MI: Kregel Publications, 1982).

----------, *101 More Stories* (Grand Rapids, MI: Kregel Publications, 1984).

Peakcock, Charlie, *At the Crossroads: An Insider's Look at the Past, Present, and Future of Contemporary Christian Music* (Nashville, TN: Broadman & Holman, 1999).

*Religious Responses to Media and Pop Culture* (1998).

*Rolling Stone Album Guide* (New York: Random House, 1992).

Tozer, A. W., *Whatever Happened to Worship?*, edited by Ged B. Smith (Camp Hill, PA: Christian Publications, 1985).

Turner, Steve, *Hungry for Heaven* (Downers Grove, IL: Intervarsity Press, 1995).

Wells, David F., *God in the Wastelands* (Grand Rapids, MI: William

B. Eerdman's, 1994).

Wheaton, Dr. Jack, *All That Jazz: A History of Afro-American Music* (Scarecrow Press).

----------, *Rock and Roll Revolution* (JCW Productions, Inc., 1980).

----------, *Technological and Sociological Influences on Jazz as an Art Form in America* (University of Michigan Press, 1976).


## Articles

"The Biology of Music, *The Economist.*

"Bibliography for Music Therapy," Mary Rikov, MA, MTA, and Deborah Salmon, MA, MTA, CMT, *The American Journal of Hospice and Palliative Care,* Vol. 15, No. 3, May/June 1998.

"Brain Anatomy and Music," *Musica Research Notes,* Vol. VI, No. 2, Spring 1999.

"Music in the Early Christian Church," John C. Andrews, *New Grove Dictionary of Music and Musicians,* ed. Stanley Sadie, Vol. 4, 1980, pp. 363–364.

"Contemporary Worship Trends," Julie Barrier, *International Resource Book for Church and School Musicians,* Church Street Press, Nashville, TN, December 1999.

"Do's and Don'ts in Hiring Pros for Church Programs," Jack Wheaton, *International Resource Book for Church and School Musicians,* December 1999.

"Healing Sounds," Jane F. Brewer, *Complentary Therapies in Nursing and Midwifery, International Journal,* Vol. 4, No. 1, April 24, 1998.

"Making Music Makes You Smarter," NAMM, 5790 Armada Dr., Carlsbad, CA 92008, e-mail: namm@namm.com.

"The History of Gospel Music," Phil Petrie, *CMM Magazine,* February 1996.

"The Mozart Effect: A Small Part of the Big Picture," *Musica Research Notes,* Vol. VII, No. 1, Winter 2000.

"Music Is Good Medicine," Marian Westley, *Newsweek,* September 21, 1998, pp. 103–104.

"Music Therapy," Jacqueline Manning, RGN, *British Journal of Theater Nursing,* Vol. 7, No. 3, June 1997.

"Music Therapy," Rick Weiss, *American Music Therapy Association,* Silver Springs, MD.

"Scientific Studies Have Proven That Music Participation Enhances Vital Intellectual Skills in Children," NAMM, Iowa Alliance for Arts Education

"The So-Called Mozart Effect May Be Just a Dream," Joanna Weiss, *Boston Globe*

"A Call for Reformation in the Contemporary Christian Music Industry," Steve Camp, a poster/essay accompanied by 107 theses made public, October 31, 1997.

"A Noebel Cause: The Constant Crusader Shares His Rhetoric on Rock," Steve Rabey, *CCM Magazine,* May 1986, pp. 23–25.

"Silver Anniversary: Maranatha!", *CCM Magazine,* November 1996.

"Your Child's Brain," Sharon Begly, *Newsweek,* February 19, 1996.

### Magazines, Periodicals

*American Music Theraphy Association, Inc.,* 8455 Colesville Rd., #1000, Silver Springs, MD 20910.

*Contemporary Christian Music,* Nashville, TN.

*Worship Leader Magazine,* 107 Kenner Ave., Nashville, TN 37205.

### CDs, Audio Tapes

*Acoustic Hymns* — classical guitar, keyboards, and small choral groups — 25 favorites

*At the Foot of the Cross* — selected artists: Amy Grant, Sandi Patti, Brian Duncan, etc.

*Cathedrals Anthology* — favorite gospel quartet — 35 years of music

*Contemporary Christian Music in the Church and in the Home* (panel), *Focus on the Family,* 1984

*Counterfeit Revival: Looking for God in All the Wrong Places,* Hank Hanegraaff (Word Audio)

*Christmas Joy,* Vol. 1 — solo piano — Dr. Jack Wheaton (Oklahoma City: Hearthstone Publishing, Ltd.)

*Favorite Hymns*, Vol. 1 — solo piano — Dr. Jack Wheaton (Oklahoma City: Hearthstone Publishing, Ltd.)

*Found a Place* — FFH — acoustic pop sound

*He Touched Me: The Gospel Music of Elvis Presley* — 2-CD set

*Hymns of Our Faith* — 4-CD collection (Christian Book Distributors)

*If That Isn't Love* — George Beverly Shea

*Maranatha: 25th Anniversary*

*Millennium Worship* — Ron Kenoly, Alvin Slaughter, etc.

*Strategic Trnds Year 2000* — Chuck Missler, (Couer d'Alene: ID: Koinonia House)

*The Best of Andrae Crouch*

*The Best of Bill Gaither and the Bill Gaither Trio*

*The Best of Carman*

*The Best of Sandi Patti*

*The Church's Music* — H. B. London, Jr., Focus on the Family Panel

*The Classics* — Ray Boltz

*The Walk* — Steven Curtis Chapman

*Wow* — worship collection from Integrity, Maranatha, and Vineyard Music

## Video Tapes

*Brooklyn Tabernacle Choir*

*Prince of Egypt* — Stephen Spielberg, producer, 1998, 99 minutes

*The New Messiah* — concert tour

*Wow 2000: The Videos* — best music from your favorite artists

# About the Author

Jack Wheaton grew up in a musical family. His father was a well-known musician in Denver, Colorado. Frank Wheaton, Jack's father played violin, guitar, and trumpet professionally, and taught those instruments as well, until he was eighty-nine years of age.

Jack began the study of piano and trumpet when he was nine years old. He went on to graduate from the University of Denver with a BA in Music in 1953. Later he finished his master's degree at the University of Northern Colorado in 1957. His final degree, a doctorate in music and history, was primarily through the University of Southern California, Los Angeles.

Dr. Wheaton was music department chairman at Cerritos College, Norwalk, California; College of the Redwoods, Eureka, California; and Administrative Director of Jazz Studies at the University of Southern California, Los Angeles. He served briefly on the faculty of the University of San Diego and has been a guest lecturer at over fifty colleges.

He has an Emmy Award for musical director for an ABC-TV Special, "Neophonic Spring," as well as directing and supervising the Gershwin segment of the 1984 Opening Ceremonies of the Olympic Games in Los Angeles. He has authored over fifteen books, his most recent, *All That Jazz: A History of Afro-American Music* and *Career Counseling for Today's Musician,* written for the American Federation of Musicians. As a composer, he has scored the musical soundtracks to eight Hollywood feature films, many jingles, and documentaries. As a pianist he is featured on seven CDs, two of the most recent being *Christmas Joy* and *Favorite Hymns* (vol 1) for Hearthstone Publishing.

His music ministry positions are many, with the most recent being the director of instrumental music for Calvary Church in Santa Ana, California, the largest church in Orange County, where he arranged for and conducted regularly a seventy-piece orchestra, as well as works for choir.

Dr. Wheaton has many published works for choir and praise band, and is currently working on an Easter cantata and an oratorio on the book of Esther. Sought after as a consultant for church music programs Jack became increasingly concerned about the growing crisis in church music; hence the authoring of this book.

For a more detailed biography and available materials and recordings consult his internet address: *www. showgigs.com/jackwheaton* or write: JCW Productions, Inc.; P.O. Box 1331; Rancho Santa Fe, CA 92067.